Dear Friends

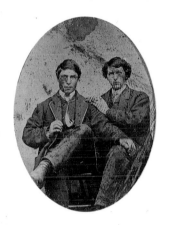

AMERICAN

PHOTOGRAPHS

OF MEN

TOGETHER,

1840–1918

Dear Friends

AMERICAN PHOTOGRAPHS OF MEN TOGETHER, 1840–1918

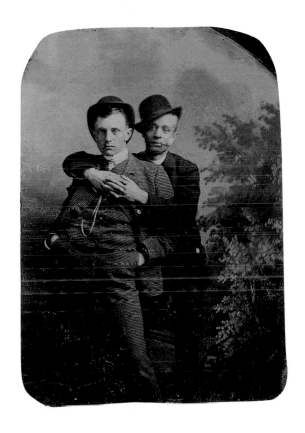

BY DAVID DEITCHER

★

HARRY N. ABRAMS, INC., PUBLISHERS

EDITOR: Elisa Urbanelli
DESIGNER: Dana Sloan
PRINCIPAL PHOTOGRAPHER: Eileen Travell

Library of Congress Cataloging-in-Publication Data
Deitcher, David.
    Dear friends: American photographs of men together, 1840–1918 / David Deitcher.
    p.   cm.
    Includes bibliographical references and index.
    ISBN 0–8109–5712–4 (hardcover) / ISBN 0–8109–2996–1 (book club pbk.)
    / ISBN 0–8109–9230–2 (trade pbk.)
    1. Gay male couples—United States—Portraits. 2. Gay men—United States—Portraits.
    3. Portrait photography—United States—History. 4. Portrait photography—Social
    aspects—United States. 5. Male friendship—United States—Pictorial works. I. Title.

TR681.H65 D45 2001
779'.23'097309034—dc21   00—062076

Trade paperback edition published in 2005 by Harry N. Abrams, Incorporated, New York
All rights reserved. No part of the contents of this book may be reproduced without
the written permission of the publisher.
Hardcover edition published in 2001 by Harry N. Abrams, Inc.

Printed and bound in China
10 9 8 7 6 5 4 3 2 1

Harry N. Abrams, Inc.
100 Fifth Avenue
New York, N.Y. 10011
www.abramsbooks.com

Abrams is a subsidiary of

LA MARTINIÈRE
G R O U P E

CONTENTS

★

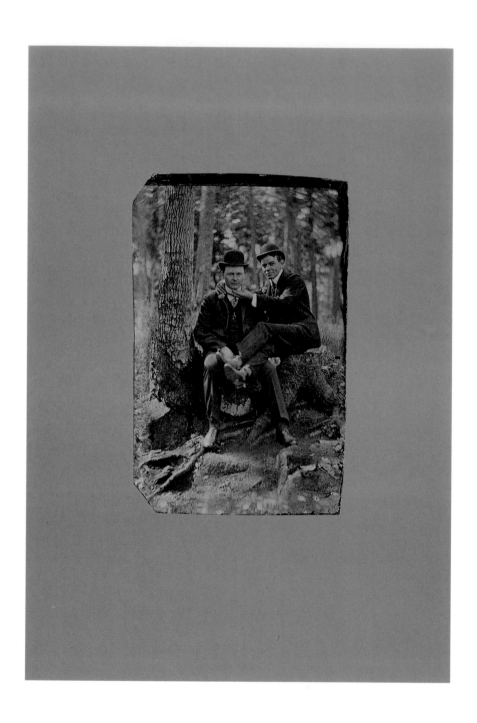

PHOTOGRAPHER UNKNOWN, SUBJECTS UNKNOWN, TINTYPE (3½ × 2½″), C. 1880

A NOTE ON
EARLY PHOTOGRAPHIC FORMATS

★

Dear Friends is intended for all readers, regardless of whether or not they are familiar with the arcana of nineteenth-century photographic techniques and formats. Nineteenth-century photography was marked by a rapidly unfolding sequence of sometimes overlapping technological developments that led from the invention of daguerreotypes and ambrotypes to the introduction of tintypes; and from the first photographic prints on paper to the commercial dissemination of multiple prints from negatives such as cartes de visites, cabinet cards, and "real photo" postcards. These developments were accompanied by evolving conventions for describing variations in the size and formats of different kinds of photographs. Today these conventions remain informative principally among specialists in early photography. The captions accompanying the reproductions in this book preserve some of those conventions, while departing from tradition in ways that warrant brief explanation.

In order to provide readers with a reasonably accurate representation of what the original photographs look like, and to convey something of the intimacy that inheres in examining such objects at first hand, an effort was made to reproduce the photographs in this book at a scale that does not depart too much from the original size. In order to ensure that readers can readily gauge the actual size of the original object, captions include its dimensions in inches, with height preceding width. Where "cased images" such as daguerreotypes and ambrotypes are reproduced to display both the left-hand panel with its velvet or satin pad as well as the panel on the right containing the photograph behind its ornamental metal preserver and mat, measurements refer to the height and width of the closed case.

This method departs from convention in more ways than one. In illustrated books and catalogues on early photography, the measurement of cased images such as daguerreotypes invariably still refers to the size of the photosensitized silver-coated copper plate, rather than that of the decorative case that would ultimately contain and protect it. Moreover, the size of a daguerreotype is not traditionally measured in inches, but is denoted instead in terms of the fraction that a given plate represents of the standard, full-size copper plate that manufacturers mass produced for distribution to photographers from the mid-1840s, thereby establishing the daguerreotype as the first commercially viable form of photography. The size of such full plates has been estimated at 8½ × 6½ inches. Smaller sizes commonly included the half plate (5½ × 4½ inches), the ¼ plate (4⅛ × 3⅛ inches), the ⅙ plate (3¼ × 2⅝ inches), the ⅑ plate (2½ × 2 inches), and the 1/16 plate (1⅝ × 1⅜ inches). These dimensions are approximate—averages, in fact—based on the dimensions of daguerreotypes that have survived. (It was not unusual for daguerreotypists to trim the mass-produced plate).* Notwithstanding its lack of universal and scientific precision, this method of referring to the size of photosensitized plates was also applied to the ambrotype (a photographic impression on glass) after its introduction in 1854. In *Dear Friends,* captions accompanying reproductions of daguerreotypes and ambrotypes preserve this fractional method of denoting plate size, but supplement it with the dimensions of the object that contains them in inches, as noted above.

The commercial manufacture and dissemination of photosensitized copper and glass plates in standardized sizes was retained as well by manufacturers of the thin iron sheets (photosensitized by a film of silver nitrate against a background of dark Japan varnish) that photographers employed in the production of tintypes after their introduction in 1856. But although manufacturers adopted this standard to mass produce and distribute such plates, photographers—many of them itinerants working at the far reaches of the continental United States out of horse-drawn wagons that might at once serve as home, studio, and darkroom—did not

---

* There are many available sources for such technical information, and not all of them agree on the fundamental details. I have relied on O. Henry Mace, *Collector's Guide to Early Photographs* (Iola, WI: Krause Publications, 1999), 20–25.

hesitate to cut and trim them to suit their immediate needs and desires. Surviving tintypes therefore exist in a bewildering array of irregular sizes and shapes, suggesting a veritable photographic folk tradition. As a result, the old fractional system for denoting the size of a photograph based on its plate size cannot meaningfully be applied to tintypes. In *Dear Friends* the captions accompanying reproductions of tintypes therefore measure the original object, as reproduced on the page, in inches alone. The same applies to captions accompanying reproductions of paper prints, whether they assume the standardized commercial form of the carte-de-visite, the cabinet card, or the real photo postcard.

ACKNOWLEDGMENTS

★

In preparing this book, I was fortunate to receive the assistance and encouragement of many friends and associates. My interest in nineteenth-century photographs of men together might never have developed at all had I not first met Craig Bruns, an artist and collector from Philadelphia who created an inspiring chapbook that includes, among other things, reproductions of old photographs of affectionate men. My interest in such photographs deepened with the guidance and encouragement of my friend Brian Wallis, whose knowledge about so many aspects of early American photography and social history has proven invaluable. I have also benefitted from the example of my friend Robert Flynt who has meaningfully incorporated early American photographs of men together into his artistic practice, and who enthusiastically spread the word about my project to other enthusiasts. Lynne Tillman brought Carole Smith-Rosenberg's important work on romantic friendship between nineteenth-century women to my attention. Daile Kaplan provided critical advice and guidance at a crucial moment in the book's preparation. Fronia Simpson helped to ensure the unity of the manuscript. And my dear friend Amy Sholder helped me to grasp the shape of the manuscript at a time when it seemed to me there was no shape at all.

Photo research—the task of hunting down pictures for possible reproduction—is never an easy matter. At a critical point in this process, I had the good fortune to contact John Wood, devoted cofounder of the Daguerreian Society of America, who kindly referred me to a number of generous collectors, and who recommended that I place a query in the society's newsletter. Without John's advice, this book would surely lack many of its most important and earliest examples.

While doing research and writing, there were people I met or corresponded with who helped the process along in many different ways: Drew Johnson and Jeffrey Kramm of the Oakland Museum of California, Vince Aletti, Fred Koszewnik, Melissa Maltby, Steven Barker, Roberto Ceriani, William Doan, Chris Gordon, Mark S. Johnson, Peter Miller, Donald Lewis Osborn, and Harry Weintraub. I am deeply grateful as well to all the collectors who not only expressed interest in this project and permitted me to reproduce their photographs in this book, but who agreed to part with their treasures, entrusting them to this total stranger for copying. The fact that those photographs were properly—no, impeccably—copied and handled is due to the remarkable work of photographer Eileen Travell. I am grateful as well to Malcolm Daniel, curator of photography at the Metropolitan Museum of Art, for directing me to her.

Elisa Urbanelli, my editor at Abrams, championed this project from its inception and kept everything on track in the most unstressful way. Dana Sloan, also at Abrams, did a wonderful job in designing the book and generously invited me to interfere in her process. I contacted Paul Gottlieb at Abrams for advice regarding where I might go to get such a book published after my friend and agent, the late Diane Cleaver, suddenly died before I could even come through with the book proposal she so much wanted to have in hand. I am deeply grateful to Paul for responding to my request for advice with the suggestion that Abrams might be interested in publishing my book. Thanks as well to my agent, Ellen Geiger at Curtis Brown, for her help in finessing so many details.

Dear Friends has also become an exhibition at the International Center of Photography through the encouragement of its chief curator, Brian Wallis. I am deeply grateful to him for making this possible. I also want to thank Kristen Lubben, curatorial assistant at the I.C.P., for her support throughout the process of realizing the exhibition.

Finally, my thanks to all those who constitute my life support system: Julie Ault, Martin Beck, Robert Bordo, and Anne Rogin. And much more than thanks to my mate, Clayton Guthrie. This book is for him.

✫   ✫   ✫

Look at this picture. What do you see? A photographic shard, a sliver of paper, measuring little more than one inch square in warm shades of gray and brown. Its lower right-hand corner is missing—broken off perhaps owing to the brittleness of such old paper—and its surface is further disfigured by a burn mark. Registered in the emulsion of this tiny silver chloride (or gelatin silver) print is a medium close-up of a pair of handsome young men. Evidently they went to the trouble of combing their hair for the photographer, but they are otherwise dressed casually in simple jackets worn over shirts with neither collars nor ties, in a style that suggests American working men of the 1890s. The fellow on the left is radiantly fair, with clear, soft eyes. His darker friend has piercing eyes and a level gaze that suggests confidence and poise. But it is the intimacy with which these men posed so long ago, and the survival of this fragile object against the odds, that makes this photograph an object of wonder to me. Each man rests a hand affectionately on the shoulder of the other; or, more precisely, at the point where the shoulder meets the bare skin of the neck. Such a comfortable display of mutual affection between men in the presence of a commercial photographer would be rare indeed in our supposedly more liberal time.

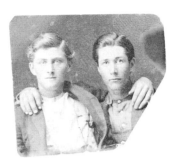

PHOTOGRAPHER UNKNOWN, SUBJECTS UNKNOWN, PRINTING-OUT PAPER PRINT (1¼ × 1¼"), C. 1890–1900

    I first became aware of photographs like those that appear throughout the pages of this book when I saw this one during the spring of 1994. I'd been invited to give a lecture at the Tyler School of Art in Elkins Park, Pennsylvania. A student there had volunteered to meet me at Philadelphia's Thirtieth-Street Station in order to drive me out to the school. My lecture concerned an incendiary topic: contemporary cultural

13

practices that demonstrate a gay, lesbian, or "queer" perspective on life. The student had a particular interest in the subject of my talk, having only just come to terms with the fact that he too is gay. After the lecture, he drove me back to the train station, and as we sat in the warm cabin of his battered Ford Ranger pickup truck, he handed me a copy of his own work-in-progress: a handsome artist's book entitled (after a poem by Walt Whitman), "Of the Terrible Doubt of Appearances." His project included reproductions of anonymous nineteenth-century photographs of men in affectionate poses, as well as more informal World War II-era snapshots of American soldiers enjoying leisure time. These he juxtaposed with fragments from a variety of published writings concerning gay history, identity, and the nature of sexual difference. Even a cursory glance through the pages of his book made it clear that the photographs and the writings it contained had been an indispensable source of pleasure, stimulation, and strength to its author throughout his solitary struggle for self-acceptance. But it was the earlier photographs, such as the tiny print of the two young men, which came as a revelation to me. This ephemeral object has survived its abandonment, just as it has survived the men whose appearance it preserves, the memory of their names, and any details about their lives except their physical appearance. These factors combined with the surprising intimacy of the anonymous sitters to trigger a powerful emotional response in me. I wanted to know more, and to see more.

Looking at these photographs has made me wonder about the kind of affection that the men in them actually shared. How was it that such men were so comfortable posing so closely together? As anonymous photographs, they remain stubbornly ambiguous objects. I know nothing about their long-since deceased subjects, nothing about the occasion that brought them together to sit for a photograph one day. A photograph like this comes with no provenance, often without even an inscription that might provide clues to help answer the many questions it raises. The Tyler student picked it up for a song at a Pennsylvania flea market, as he did the other old pictures he's collected. One thing I know: He was powerfully drawn to these objects, believing that in them he had found something that he wanted, and even needed, to see.

Being drawn in this way to enigmatic artifacts from the past provides evidence of longing: longing for the self-validation that results from having a history to refer to; longing for a comforting sense of connection to others—past as well as present—whose experience mirrors one's own.

Inasmuch as photographs like this lack supporting documentation, they are powerless to communicate anything more than the following: This is how these men looked on that day when they sat for the photographer. Anonymity, and the uncertainty it perpetuates, facilitate a kind of pleasure that would be more difficult to sustain under the potentially harsh, and always more limiting, details of a more concrete historical intelligence. Research into the gay history of nineteenth-century London prompted one writer to ask: "Do we view it with dismay, since it is a record of sorrow, of powerlessness, a record of lives wrecked? Or is it possible to read even these texts, written as they were by journalists, policemen and court clerks, with delight, as precious traces of dangerous, pleasurable, complicated gay lives?"[1] Uncertain of anything that ever actually transpired between the men in such a photograph, the collector is free to imagine whatever he pleases. Immersed in their appearance, he remains

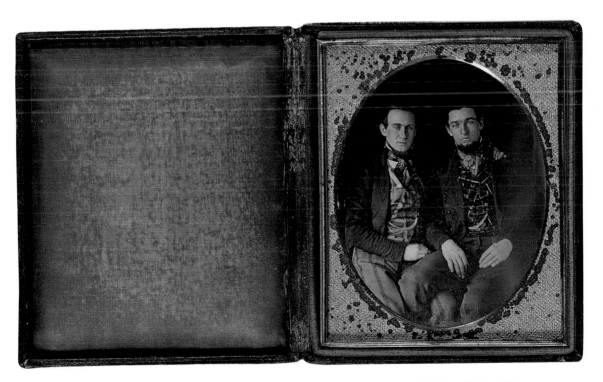

PHOTOGRAPHER UNKNOWN, SUBJECTS UNKNOWN, 1/4-PLATE DAGUERREOTYPE (4 1/2 × 3 5/8 "), C. 1845–50

ignorant of any tragedy that might have befallen them, or of any crime they may have committed or been punished for. With neither caption nor context to anchor this object of his desire, he is free to wonder: By what hazardous, indirect route did this uncanny image, imprinted on a fragile scrap of paper, survive to find its way to my desk, where it arouses curiosity about the details of the world it so vividly pictures, and desire for whatever it represents?

Such a relation to photographs of anonymous men is therefore akin to flirtation. It parallels the sense of limitless possibility that depends on not knowing very much more about a man than is suggested by his presence, and on deferring the moment of defining the nature of an erotic relationship that may be sexual but that cannot be "fixed" in the sense that committed relationships are. Desire thrives on the suggestion, on the possible, just as surely as it shrinks from the light of a deeper familiarity. British psychoanalyst Adam Phillips has written that flirtation "sustains the life of desire." As in flirtation, the collector's desire to sustain a relationship with these photographs and to the men they record embraces uncertainty as "a way of cultivating wishes, of playing for time."[2]

In looking at old photographs of anonymous men, desire ranges freely, attracted to the quirks of physical appearance as well as the appearance of intimacy; to a man's looks, comportment, and style, which antiquity renders especially alluring. I find myself drawn to a broader range of physical types than is the case today: to skinny men with odd, angular faces; to men with crudely cut, heavily pomaded, or just plain greasy hair; to unshaven men and to men who sport extravagant sideburns, handlebar mustaches, or full shaggy beards. It would be hard to exaggerate the contrast between the men in these pictures and today's masculine ideal of chiseled features and gym-crafted bodies suggesting armor, not flesh; imagined as if in cybernetic resistance to aging or plague.

It is as if men put themselves together more inventively back then. Notwithstanding the legibility of codified fashions among borderline dandies like the men in some of these pictures, other men in other pictures responded with a combination of invention and pragmatism to the varied circumstances of nineteenth-century and early-twentieth-century life, as members of different classes in variously urban, rural, and frontier settings. American men of disparate economic means evolved styles of dress and modes of comportment that, in retrospect, seem strikingly original. But perhaps this is too distanced, too abstract a way of looking, which

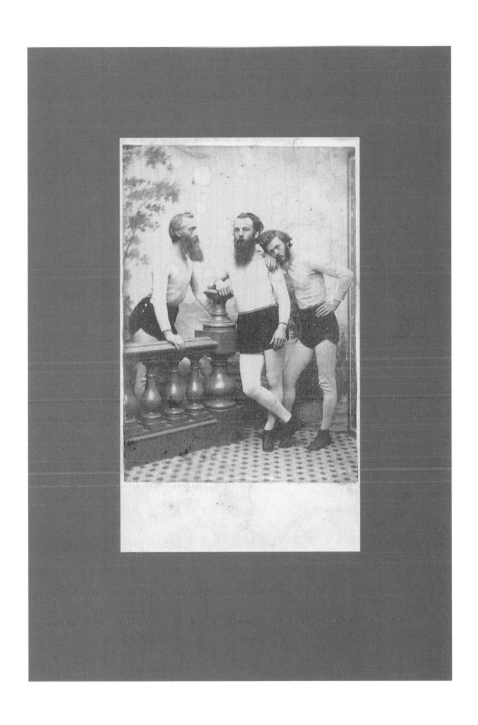

GEORGE M. HOWE, CARTE DE VISITE (4¹/₄ × 2¹/₂″), C. 1865. BACKMARK ON VERSO READS:
"GEORGE M. HOWE, 'SPECIALITE,' 112 MIDDLE STREET, PORTLAND, ME."

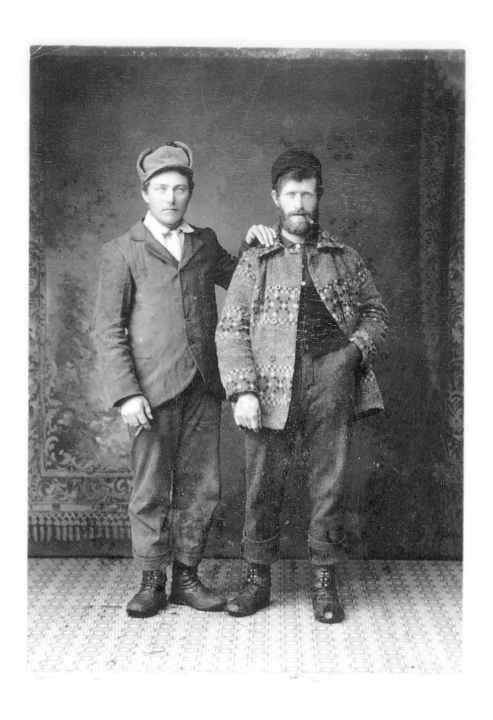

PHOTOGRAPHER UNKNOWN, SUBJECTS UNKNOWN, CABINET CARD
(TRIMMED: 6½ × 4⅛"), C. 1885. "LAATSCH/MERRILL, WIS."

depends too much on the knowledge that so much about their style has since been codified, copied, and reified by today's purveyors of masculine American style, from Hollywood to Marlboro to Ralph Lauren.

In addition to the mildly erotic pleasures of looking at affectionate men from another time, there are other factors that draw me to these old photographs. I am drawn to the orphaned picture—to the castoff that lies unnoticed and undignified at the weekend flea market amid the unsorted elastic-bound stacks of other tintypes, cartes-de-visite, and postcards. I feel something other than exhilaration in having discovered photographic evidence of historic same-sex affection in an era of possibly more fluid relations. I identify with the weathered object. In its tears, scuff marks, and dents, I see the signs of age, and more. I see the stigmata of their abandonment and mistreatment as so much discarded junk. To be drawn so empathetically to inanimate objects suggests a form of identification with them; that, and a decidedly morbid relation to the past.

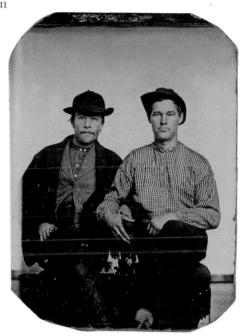

Like most photographs, these old likenesses convey a vivid sensation of the presence of the sitters who died long ago. The morbid pleasure in look- ing at them results, in part, from certain characteristics of photography itself, which Roland Barthes, among other writers, has noted. Looking at this object, I am aware that long ago light registered its uncanny impression in the emulsion-coated surface as it probed

PHOTOGRAPHER UNKNOWN, SUBJECTS UNKNOWN, TINTYPE (3½ × 2½"), C. 1875

the living bodies of these men in their space and time at the instant of exposure. Just as the passage of time has stripped these men of their identities, so exposure to light, which brought their image into being and now makes them visible, is causing them to fade from view.

Are some individuals more susceptible than others to interacting with old photographs in this way? I've long considered that gay men hold a special franchise on this dismal sense of beauty. Perhaps knowing

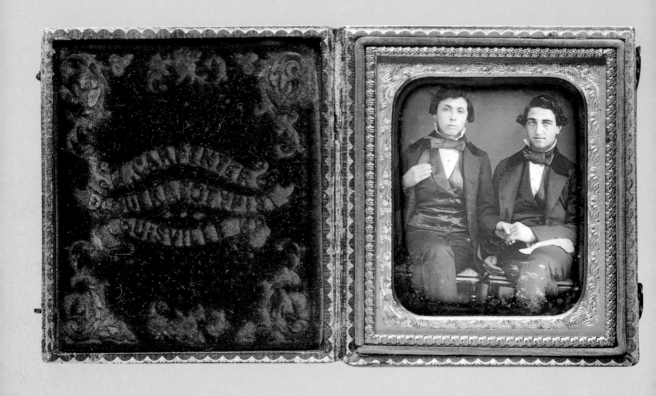

MARION CARPENTER, SUBJECTS UNKNOWN, ⅙-PLATE DAGUERREOTYPE (3¾ × 3¼", CASE), C. 1855–56.
IMPRINT ON VELVET PAD READS: "M. CARPENTER/DAGUERREOTYPIST/LOUISVILLE,KY"

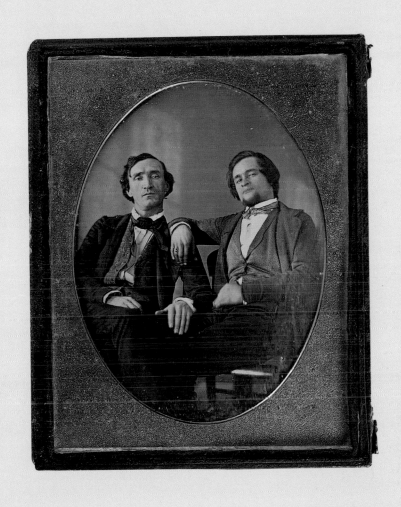

DAVID A. ROSS & CO., SUBJECTS UNKNOWN, ¼-PLATE DAGUERREOTYPE (4½ × 3½"), C. 1850–52. IMPRINT
ON SILK PAD READS: "D. A. ROSS/DAGUERREAN GALLERY/244 WEST 6TH STREET,/CIN, O."

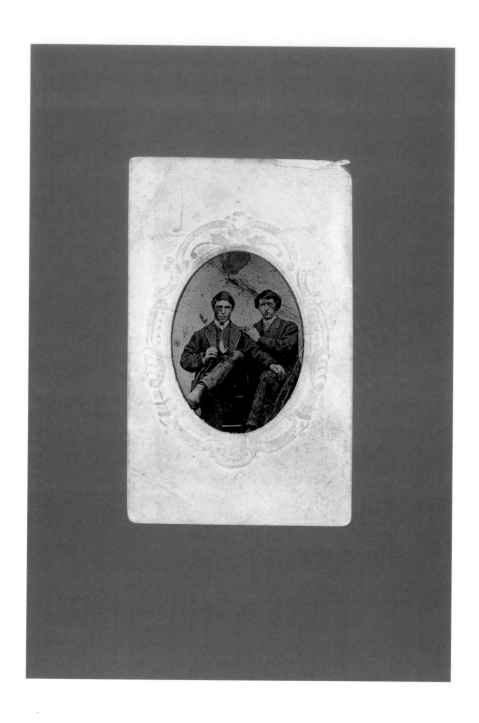

PHOTOGRAPHER UNKNOWN, SUBJECTS UNKNOWN, TINTYPE IN PAPER SLEEVE (OVERALL: 3³/₄ × 2¹/₈″), C. 1865

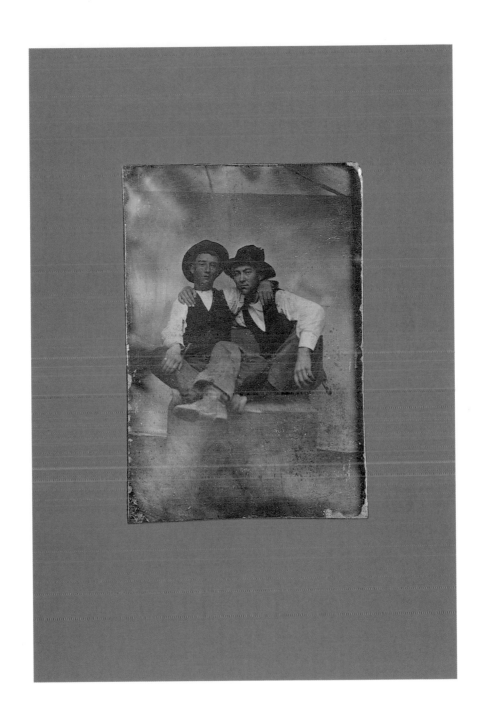

PHOTOGRAPHER UNKNOWN, SUBJECTS UNKNOWN, TINTYPE (3½ × 2½″), C. 1880

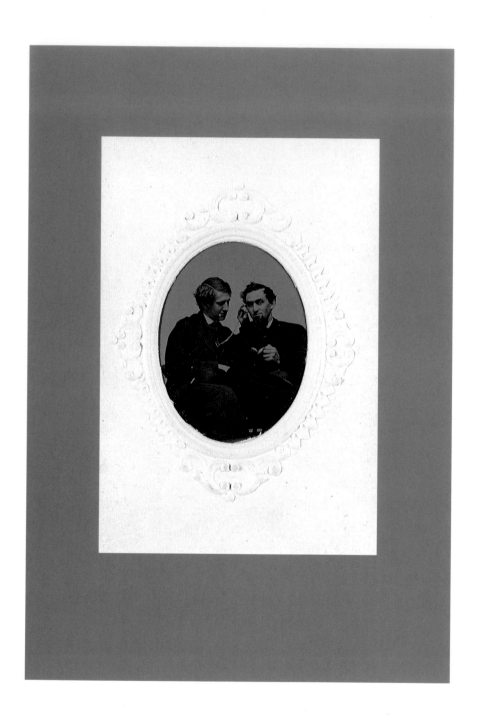

PHOTOGRAPHER UNKNOWN, SUBJECTS UNKNOWN, TINTYPE IN PAPER SLEEVE (OVERALL: 4 × 2¹/₂"), C. 1865

that no children of my own will survive to remember me contributes to my morbid attraction to these mementos of forgotten men, caught in a moment of intimate connection; as does the suspicion that some of my eight nieces and nephews may forget me too. Who among them, I wonder, will neglect to tell their children about their queer uncle David who went away and lived with a man and didn't have any children?

Sometimes I'm afraid that I glimpse my future in the past lives of those other men. But then I remember the reaction of my friend Lauren, a single straight woman in her thirties, as she leafed through a stack of these photographs while sitting on a porch on a summer day. At first she expressed delight and interest in seeing so much evidence of the physical ease and affection that American men once demonstrated together. But then she paused, as if also overcome by darker feelings. "These are sad," she added, "they're like death, aren't they?" Without knowing it, Lauren had approximated an observation that Susan Sontag once famously made about photographs: that as such vivid encapsulations of something that once was and is no more, photographs are infused with the spirit of death.

☆　　☆　　☆

In July 1997, I came upon a reproduction of a daguerreo-type of two men in the pages of the *New York Times*. In the photograph, the more handsome of the two men is seated, and the other is standing with a hand resting comfortably on the shoulder of his mate. What can one learn from the visual evidence alone? That the standing figure was perhaps of more than average height, with a lanky build and strong, weathered hands that suggest an active, physical life. He had a cleft chin, long wavy hair, a trim beard, and a pinched expression. Both men appear rugged, yet prosperous in suits worn over silk vests, clean shirts, and ties. The seated man was powerfully built, his face marked by prominent cheek bones, deep-set clear eyes that are set wide apart, and a broad, sensual mouth. He appears to be wearing some kind of headband, which combines with his short, curly hair and symmetrical features to give him a vaguely classical look. The fact that I encountered this photograph as a captioned illustration in a newspaper article meant that I did not have to rely on the testimony of the picture at all; that I could not for long enjoy the unfettered freedom to imagine whatever I pleased about the men it portrayed. A glance at the photograph's caption and the article's headline informed me about the identity of both sitters, and helped me to surmise something about the nature of the bond they shared.

The caption identified them as Texas cattle barons Richard King and Mifflin Kenedy, who posed for the half-plate daguerreotype in Brownsville in the 1850s. The article informed me that this was only a few years after the United States annexed Texas; and forcibly persuaded Mexico to sign the Treaty of Guadalupe Hidalgo. That treaty honored Mexican land titles in principle but could not guarantee them in fact, which led to tensions between Mexican landowners and the horde of American businessmen, squatters, and ex-soldiers who arrived with claims to land that may or may not have been authentic. It was in that avaricious postwar setting that King and Kenedy, like other large ranching families, consolidated their holdings. It is therefore possible that what this daguerreotype commemorates is that consolidation of wealth and power.

King and Kenedy were representative of a class of men who were so powerful that they could pretty much take possession of whatever they thought was theirs, whether or not it legally belonged to them. Hence the title of the *Times* article: "Cattle Barons of Texas Yore Accused of Epic Land Grab," which was published on the occasion of a lawsuit filed by descendants of José Manuel Balli Villarreal and his wife, Maria Antonia Cavazos de Hinojosa. In the early nineteenth century, the king of Spain deeded the disputed 363,000 acres to Balli Villarreal, whose descendants leased it to Kenedy, who then may effectively have stolen it to amass enormous wealth, not only from cattle ranching but from oil and gas that were discovered on the property.[3]

Does familiarity with potentially incriminating details about the lives of such men neutralize the attraction that I know I can sustain under the speculative conditions of a more purely imaginary association? Knowing about the underhanded and perhaps brutal behavior of someone who is the object of my desire may make me feel ashamed of that attraction, but hardly eradicates it. Indeed, the contents of my fantasies and dreams tell me that quite the contrary is true. Nevertheless, as is so often the case, I was effectively raised to pay a psychological price for such pleasurable desires in the turmoil and guilt that accompanies them.

In the "Calamus" section of *Leaves of Grass*, in "Of the Terrible Doubt of Appearances," Walt Whitman addressed the anxiety and excitement that accompanies the emotional gamble of trusting one's good first impressions of another, knowing how ill-founded such first impressions

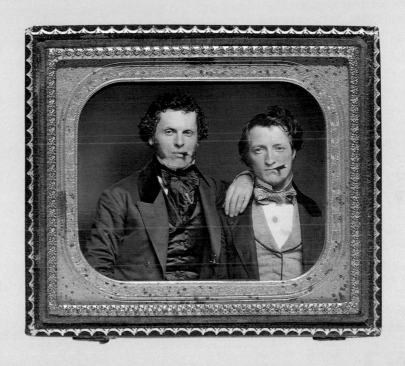

PHOTOGRAPHER UNKNOWN, SUBJECTS UNKNOWN, 1/6-PLATE DAGUERREOTYPE (3 1/4 × 3 3/4"), C. 1850–55

can ultimately prove to be. Whitman's poem also describes the gloom that sets in at the mere thought of relinquishing such admittedly uncertain trust for the safer, but emotionally deadening presumption that, as he writes, "we may be deluded." The poet's determination to suspend such disbelief acknowledges the impossibility of living in a state of permanent disillusionment, an impossibility that is shared by the gay man who searches through piles of old photographs for evidence of a past with which he can identify. Though well aware of the dangerous likelihood that "reliance and hope are but speculations after all," the poet settles on the life-affirming hopefulness of the largely imaginary sense of connection.

> *May-be seeming to me what they are (as doubtless they*
> *indeed but seem) as from my present point of view,*
> *and might prove (as of course they would) nought of*
> *what they appear, or nought anyhow, from entirely*
> *changed points of view.*[4]

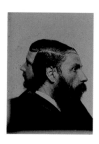

PHOTOGRAPHER
UNKNOWN, SUBJECTS
UNKNOWN, GEM TIN-
TYPE (1 × ¾"), C. 1880

I experience a parallel sense of uneasiness in deciding to bracket off whatever "history" may have to say about these photographs in order to explore what they *represent* from my decidedly interested perspective; knowing, as Whitman did, that any single vantage point can only offer a form of intelligence that is profoundly contingent. This is therefore an argument for the importance not just of documentary research, with its promise of "objective" historical knowledge, but of trusting that the attentive pursuit of subjective desires that are shaped and fueled by the emotional inner life of the mind can yield other truths of no lesser importance. Inasmuch as these photographs of men ultimately remain enigmatic objects, they attest to the desire and doubt that together motivate historical research. But by the same token, they remain humble reminders that the past cannot be recaptured—at least not through the empirical methods of modern histories that emphasize the separation between historical subjects and objects.

✴   ✴   ✴

After returning to New York, I showed the Tyler student's project to my friends and told them about my new interest in the oldest of the photographs it reproduced. Two of them responded by showing me similar photographs that they too had obtained at weekend flea markets and antique photo fairs. One friend, who is familiar with the most esoteric reaches of the antique photo world, then acquired an extraordinary photograph of the kind I had already come to regard as a significant, and significantly overlooked, aspect of American portrait photography. While the Tyler student's photographs initially opened my eyes to the existence of this practice in the United States, my friend's new acquisition revealed just how intimate such photographs could be. In this way, it raised the stakes in attempting to answer the many questions that looking at such old photographs raised.

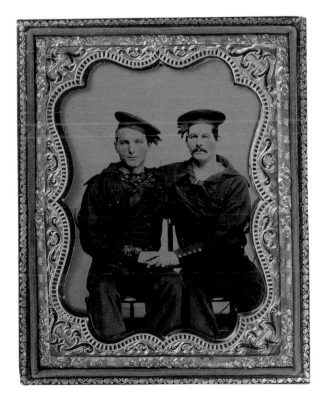

PHOTOGRAPHER UNKNOWN, SUBJECTS UNKNOWN, ¼-PLATE AMBROTYPE (4½ × 3½"), C. 1865

Here is that picture. What do you see? An ambrotype—a photograph on glass—that is secured in its red morocco case by an ornamental metal preserver and mat opposite a red velvet pad. One man, the taller one, has eyes as clear as ice but not so cold. He sits on a wooden stool, inclining to his left and slightly forward to drape a lanky arm around the neck of his friend who sits below and before him in a cane-seated chair. This leaves his hand hanging rather low against the torso of his mate, its index finger aligned with his comrade's groin in a way that I'm inclined to read as deliberate, as if to say, You know what we're about. Casually crossed legs sheathed to the knees in leather riding boots obscure all but a few suggestive folds at his breeches' buttoned fly. This seated man has taken the third finger and pinkie of his companion's suspended hand inside his own as he looks at the camera with disarming directness.

The two men look relaxed, comfortable together; especially the seated one, who projects poise in the shelter of his friend's encircling body. It's hard to tell—old photographs like this ambrotype concentrate such a wealth of detail into such small objects—but his eyes look somewhat darker and softer. This much I plainly see: he wears his wavy hair pushed back from an "intelligent" brow. His right forearm rests easily between his friend's crossed thighs, his hand cupping the contour of the knee that is raised. There, his pinkie deviates ever so slightly from its neighbors—a dainty departure that nonetheless is consistent with the overall attitude of both men, which is urbane, sophisticated, even patrician.

Have I said in so many words how elegant they look in their nicely tailored sack coats? Though both men wear vests, only that of the fellow in the foreground is visible. Its brass buttons are mostly unfastened to reveal a white shirt beneath, its standing collar offset by a substantial cravat. Of the taller man's vest and shirt I discern barely a hint, because the forward inclination and inward curve of his body have combined with the more abundant folds of his generously bowed tie to conceal these garments. Who are these two men, looking out across time from the other side of a sliver of glass? When was it that they dressed for the photographer? The style of their clothes suggests the mid- to late 1850s, which corresponds with the relatively brief life of the ambrotype. The sense of leisurely style that both men exude is supported by their hands, which look soft, though manly in their mass. Fingernails as immaculate and carefully trimmed as these rule out manual labor. Neither wears a ring or any other item of jewelry, yet clearly theirs was not a Spartan life. Did they have money at birth? Or did

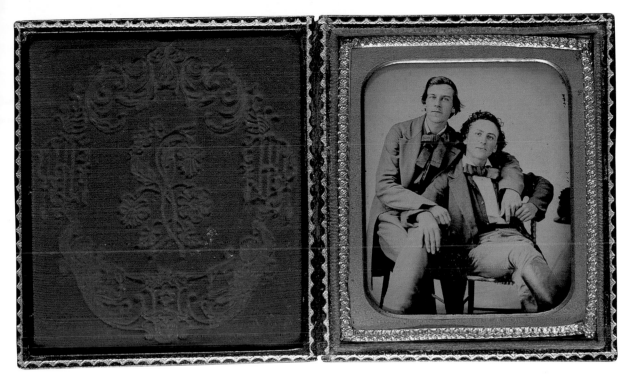

PHOTOGRAPHER UNKNOWN, SUBJECTS UNKNOWN, ⅙-PLATE AMBROTYPE (3¾ × 3¼"), C. 1860

they earn whatever money they have? Were they businessmen? Shopkeepers? Poets or journalists? Did they read Melville, Hawthorne, Emerson, Whitman?

Having seen more than a few old photographs in which nineteenth-century American men posed together with noteworthy affection, I had reason to believe that this was not an unusual practice. I began to conduct research into the history of American friendship, masculinity, and sexuality to familiarize myself with the social factors that made such photographs possible. I soon learned that the introduction of photography to the United States in 1840 coincided with what we now understand was a surprisingly broad-minded attitude toward same-sex intimacy. American men and women were in many ways encouraged to establish intense, even passionate, bonds of friendship with members of their own sex. Middle-class women, for example, formed a distinct world of love and ritual, one that was parallel to, but separate from, the relations they maintained with men. Frequently fostered in all-girl academies, these ties could be romantic, sometimes in ways that we would identify

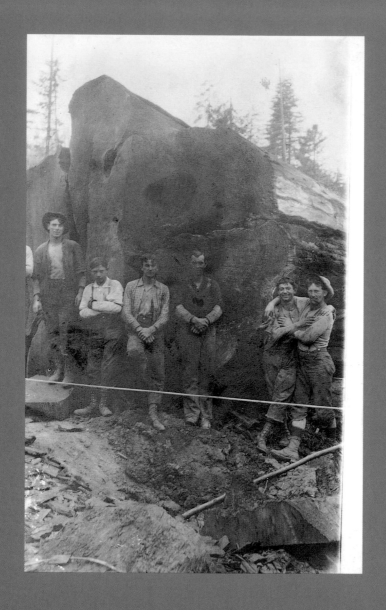

PHOTOGRAPHER UNKNOWN, SUBJECTS UNKNOWN, GELATIN SILVER PRINT,
REAL PHOTO POSTCARD (5$\frac{1}{2}$ × 3$\frac{1}{2}$″), C. 1915.

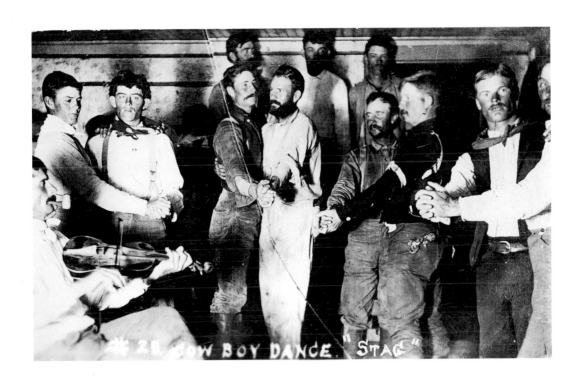

PHOTOGRAPHER UNKNOWN, SUBJECTS UNKNOWN, GELATIN SILVER PRINT, REAL PHOTO POSTCARD
(3½ × 5½"), C. 1910. INSCRIPTION IN THE NEGATIVE READS: "# 28. COWBOY 'DANCE STAG'."
POSTMARKED ON VERSO: "WINNER, S. DAK., OCT 20, [ILLEG.]"

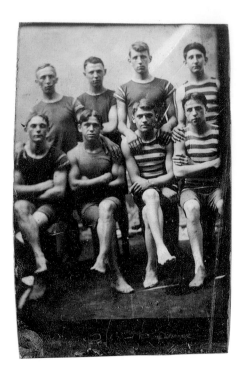

PHOTOGRAPHER UNKNOWN, SUBJECTS UNKNOWN, TINTYPE (3½ × 2¼"), C. 1890

as sexual, but that Victorians, in their state of pre-Freudian "innocence," would not. Intimate bonds between men likewise flourished in all-male havens of middle-class privilege such as the university, as well as in more socioeconomically mixed or largely working-class milieus such as the military, the merchant marine, fraternal organizations, the expanding national frontiers, and in cities to which young men raised in rural and small-town settings migrated in search of employment. The American "cult of friendship" also prompted a wide range of literary expressions, extending from private diaries and correspondence to Emerson's and Thoreau's scholastic meditations; from Melville's alternately voluptuous and agitated same-sex fictional scenarios to Walt Whitman's tireless advocacy of "comradely love," whether in impassioned poems or more sober prose in which he prescribed "manly love" as a tonic alternative to the vulgar materialism and competitiveness that dominated so much of American life. Given this background, I found it tempting to regard old photographs of affectionate men as a reflection of more fluid romantic relations. At first, I saw no reason why I should not regard them as evidence of the kind of history that I, like the Tyler student, wanted to find.

The truth, however, has proven to be a great deal more complex than that.

While conducting research into the social history of American photography, male friendship, and masculinity, I also began to search more aggressively for other examples of intimate portraits of men. I began by asking my friends for leads, and this rippled out to other leads within the relatively small community of enthusiastic devotees in and around New York City. Most of these collectors were as generous in helping me realize my project as they were eager to show me their own cherished finds. Not all, however, were so forthcoming.

Late on a spring night in 1998, I was speaking on the telephone with a prominent collector of early American photographs. I'd approached him to find out if he had any noteworthy examples of the kind of photographs I was looking for, and whether he'd be willing to show them to me. Without hesitating, he indicated his familiarity with such nineteenth-century imagery, as well as with the sociohistorical preconditions for such photographs. I was encouraged by his forthcoming response and heartened by his offer to look through his extensive holdings for pertinent examples. All I had to do was to send him e-mail reminders from time to time—not an unreasonable request considering how often this collector is approached with requests from individuals and institutions.

But things took a turn for the worse during our conversation when he noted (by way of clarification?) that the same-sex affection that such photographs record was, of course, "legitimate." I realized that in this way the collector was trying to make sure I shared his understanding that such photographs do not provide evidence of the kind of same-sex affection he evidently would consider "illegitimate." Apparently he wanted neither to aid nor abet what he suspected might be my gay historical agenda. To this day, I regret that I never took issue with him, never confronted the man with the bigoted implications of his remark. I suppose I was caught off guard, was afraid of what might happen should I reveal too much about myself to him. I'm embarrassed that I was willing to squelch whatever anger I felt at the time in order to get what I wanted from him. If that was the case, consider it a cruel and instructive irony that my passivity got me precisely nowhere. The collector never did respond to any of my e-mailed reminders. Nor would this be the only time in my dealings with collectors and historians that I would be made to feel cowardly in the face of potential disapproval from total strangers.

At a certain point in the process of conducting photo research, I reached an impasse. I'd been unable to locate a sufficient number of photographs dating from the earlier years in American photography, the 1840s and 1850s. At the advice of a friend, I phoned a well-known authority on early photographs in general, and on daguerreotypes in particular. After giving me the names and addresses of a handful of collectors and dealers he thought might have what I was looking for, he told me about the extensive community of early-photography enthusiasts who had come together as members of an organization known as The Daguerreian Society. He suggested I place a query in the *Daguerreian Society Newsletter*, which I did—taking care, as he advised, to describe my project discreetly, which is to say without any allusion to its possibly gay point of view. Soon after the newsletter arrived in the mail in February 1999, an inundation of correspondence from "daguerreians" throughout the United States made it apparent that I'd hit the mother lode. More than twenty individuals wrote me with interest, often enclosing in their correspondence reproductions of early photographs in their possession that they considered representative of what my query referred to as "comradeship."

After the query appeared, my contact with one delightful man from Missouri eventually helped me realize the extent to which my dealings with collectors like him had been tainted all along by my own internalized homophobia. It was homophobic self-censorship, masked as strategic discretion, that led me, even after people responded to my query, to describe my project to them in the disinterested manner of a scholarly photo historian. In introductory conversations, I always managed to avoid describing the nature of the desire these photographs elicited in me. Rather than admit to their emotional and erotic resonance as historic representations of same-sex love, I maintained an academic attitude, preferring to dwell instead on the "historic mutability" of friendship and masculinity.

The man from Missouri had sent me color Xeroxes of a number of interesting photographs, including a fine daguerreotype and several good tintypes. He didn't want to ship the original photographs to me, as other collectors had been willing to do, and therefore arranged to have a professional photographer copy them where he lives. When the transparencies were ready, he called. "Instead of mailing them," he suggested, "why don't I bring them to you in person?" I offered to pay him for shipping the transparencies, but he was adamant. "We've gone through all this trouble to get these things made, and I'm a retired airline employee so airfare's no problem. Besides," he added, "my daughter lives in New York."

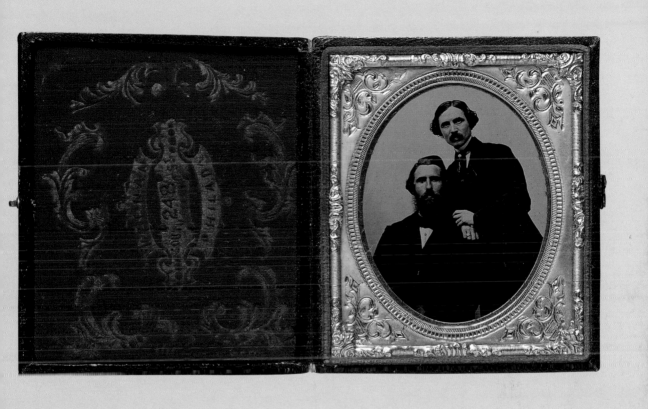

JOHN A. KEENAN, SUBJECTS UNKNOWN, 1/6-PLATE AMBROTYPE (3 1/2 × 3 1/8"), C. 1852–57.
IMPRINT ON VELVET PAD READS: "KEENAN/248 SOUTH SECOND ST./PHILADA."

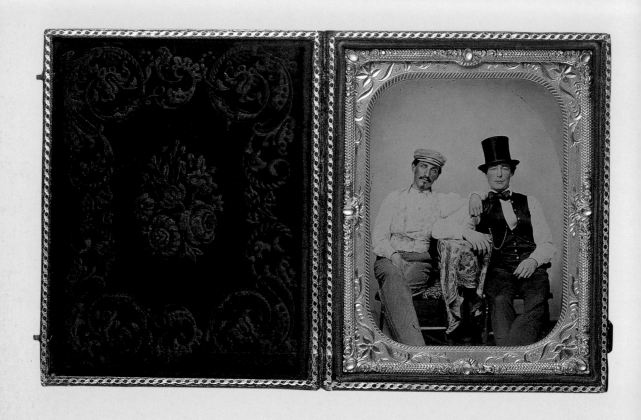

PHOTOGRAPHER UNKNOWN, SUBJECTS UNKNOWN, ¼-PLATE AMBROTYPE (4⅝ × 3⅝"), C. 1865

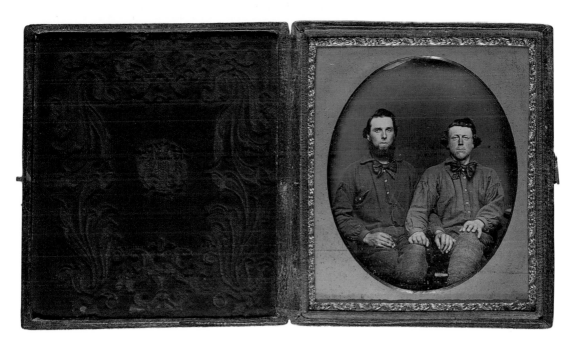

PHOTOGRAPHER UNKNOWN, SUBJECTS UNKNOWN. ⅙-PLATE DAGUERREOTYPE (3¾ × 3¼″), C. 1850

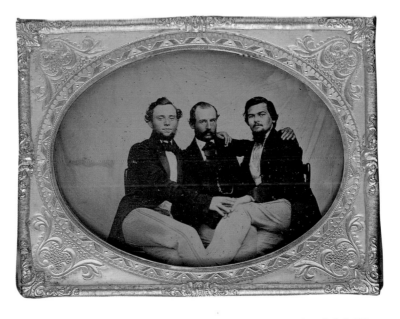

PHOTOGRAPHER UNKNOWN, SUBJECTS UNKNOWN. ⅙-PLATE AMBROTYPE (3⅜ × 3⅞″), C. 1860

A few days later, a tall, thin retiree walked into my apartment—a little gingerly, he pointed out, because of a recent hip replacement. He had a long, pleasant face, a ruddy complexion, a shock of silver hair, and a slow smile that suited his midwestern drawl. I led him into my workroom, and while I examined his photographer's handiwork I encouraged him to look over copies of the other photographs that I'd pinned up. The sight of all these photographs clearly pleased him, but then what "daguerreian" would not be happy to see scores of interesting old pictures?

As we were preparing to leave for lunch, my partner came out of the room in which he'd been working. I introduced them, and they exchanged polite greetings. But outside, as the collector and I were walking to a nearby diner, he turned to me and said, "I don't mean to pry, but

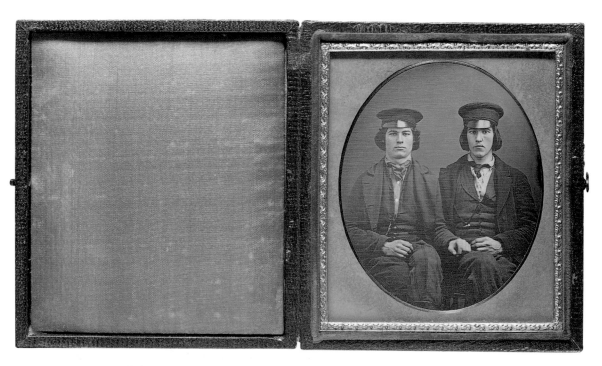

PHOTOGRAPHER UNKNOWN, SUBJECTS UNKNOWN, 1/6-PLATE DAGUERREOTYPE (3³/₄ × 3¹/₄"), C. 1845–48

was that young man you introduced me to your partner?" I answered yes, adding that we've been together for seventeen years. He congratulated me and then added that he and his wife were married in 1960. "We had two children and then unexpectedly she died of leukemia. I'm very proud," he said, "of having raised two fine young people as a single gay dad." A single *gay* dad? That this came as something of a shock to me was itself more surprising than anything that the man had actually said. All along I'd assumed that he was straight, an assumption that he'd reinforced inadvertently by mentioning the daughter he planned to visit while in New York. I assumed he was straight, despite the fact that he shared my interest in nineteenth-century images of male affection. I'd clung to that assumption rather than relinquish an intractable pair of homophobic myths: first, that men who marry must be straight; second, that parenting is an exclusively heterosexual prerogative.

Given the increasing number of lesbians and gay men raising children these days, and the legions of married men and women who had always engaged in more or less furtive gay sexual encounters, it seemed irrational to be continuing to identify marriage and childrearing exclusively with heterosexuality. Even as a boy, I'd learned with the unwitting help of my parents (of all people) to question those alibis. When I was a child, I remember that my mother worshipped Leonard Bernstein. One night at the dinner table, she was holding forth on the subject of the charismatic conductor when, out of nowhere, in a fit of competitive pique, my father pronounced her beloved Lenny a fag. To this outrage my mother responded that the maestro was—thank you very much—a happily married father. A smirk momentarily disturbed the symmetry of my father's face, who needed to say no more since my mother's defense of her idol had struck him as the non sequitur I later knew it to be.

And yet, even the thought that the men in these photographs might have married and raised children is dismaying to me. As my research into the social history of male friendship in the United States has revealed, the naturalized identification of marriage and parenting with heterosexuality has often been used to deny the queer past. Countless gay men and lesbians have been coerced into acquiescing in this conspiracy of self-denial. Given how commonplace it has been for same-sexers to lead double lives, and the force of the terror that has fueled this masquerade, universal heterosexuality seems a more convenient than fitting conclusion to draw from the matrimonial glut.

Dismay, under any circumstances, is a strong and troubling emotion, one that leaves a sense of depletion and powerlessness in its wake. But what does it mean to experience dismay in reflecting on the historical probability that the men in these photographs may well have married and had children? The feeling surfaces as if in acknowledgment of the many men and women who have been coerced into living a lie, having had little choice but to assist in expunging their deviant desires from the historical record. But to the extent that dismay is also a form of abjection, it suggests deeper roots than mere frustration in the search for signs of a past that has been obscured. I feel the disabling effects of dismay when, for example, I read historical accounts of romantic friendship between men that conclude (as if to eliminate the possibility that these intimate same-sex ties may have also been sexual) that they ended with adulthood and marriage—the two, inevitably, being equated. The historian Anthony Rotundo drew this conclusion in his study of romantic friendships, passionate attachments that he limited to the interregnum between boyhood and manhood. In romantic friendship, he observed, nineteenth-century youths found a substitute for the "emotional nurture provided most often in boyhood by a mother," the "worldly counsel" supplied by a father, even "a rehearsal for marriage."[5]

Defining adulthood and maturity in terms of marriage and successful adaptation to the harshly competitive, male-dominated nineteenth-century workplace, Rotundo implied that any man who married but nonetheless sustained a romantic friendship suffered from arrested development, to say nothing of those other men who never married, including those who, in the face of draconian punishment, participated in illicit same-sex relations. Such a view is consistent, of course, with the view of homosexuals as psychologically arrested narcissists, Peter Pans who have failed successfully to navigate the oedipal shoals. This painfully familiar scenario was upheld by the homophobic postwar vulgarizers of Freud's problematic etiology of homosexual object choice.[6] Dismay—at the absence of history where history should be, at the intractability and apparent logic of the homophobic mind-set—may therefore be rage turned inward, partly in fear of the annihilating force of that violent emotion, partly in frustration at being intimidated at the thought of the real and imagined destructive power that has almost succeeded in supplanting the queer past with the popular myth that no such past exists. Dismay of this kind is a self-fulfilling sense of one's own powerlessness.

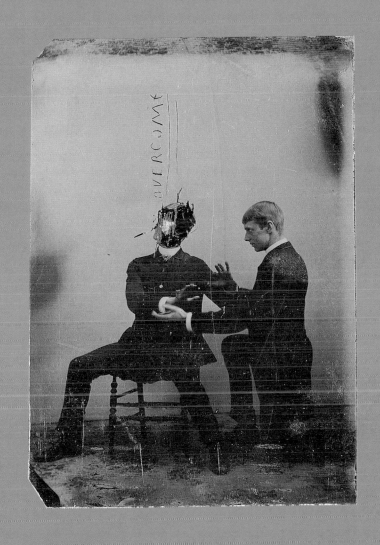

PHOTOGRAPHER UNKNOWN, SUBJECTS UNKNOWN, TINTYPE (3⅜ × 2⅜"), C. 1890.
INCISED ABOVE DEFACED FIGURE: "OVERCOME"

Only over lunch with the man from Missouri was I finally able to discuss freely the nature of my interest in old photographs of men together. Until then, I had believed that such forthrightness would jeopardize my chances of securing the cooperation of collectors. And yet, with the exception of the collector who promised to respond to my e-mail reminders but never did, only one other man came close to justifying those fears. "In response to your call for images of male affection," his e-mail began, "I might be inclined to submit an image or two but am curious as to the light in which they would be presented. Is the object of your book to indicate a homosexual affection (which I believe 99% of such images are not) or just to illustrate the differences in the manner [in] which men/boys interacted with each other 150 years ago?" Weeks passed before I responded by writing that while it was not my intention to claim such photographs as proof of a gay past, I fully intended to consider "how and why such ambiguous artifacts stimulate different responses in different viewers—including those who are homosexual and might want to find evidence of a past with which they can identify." I was genuinely surprised when this collector provided me with access to an extremely elegant daguerreotype of two youths who may or may not have been brothers. Each of them has extended an arm around the other's shoulder, and both have reached the other arm forward to clasp hands before them. The result is an elliptical composition that is echoed by the daguerreotype's oval mat. More than any other photograph reproduced here, I think of this one as epitomizing the specifically youthful affection that, according to Rotundo, would disappear as soon as these boys grew up to be men.

But what about the many surviving photographs of similarly affectionate men who were fully grown when their pictures were taken? Are such photographs and the commemorative tradition they exemplify representative of a time when same-sex love was freer and less fraught than it later became? Do such photographs provide evidence of a time when impassioned ties between men, and between women, were taken for granted—or, perhaps more precisely, taken *as* granted? Are they surviving shards from a past that, from a certain perspective, looks positively Arcadian, inasmuch as—given a certain discretion—the intimate relations they picture, and others that they only imply, were for some time spared the all-encompassing suspicion and scorn that would later be heaped upon them? But what kind of Arcadia is it that brackets off as "unspeakable" some of

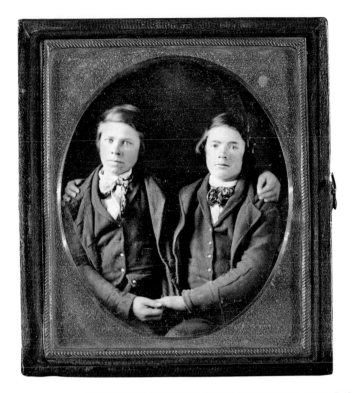

the most intimate forms of human contact? Might such pictures simply
reflect that prevalence in the nineteenth century of loving feelings between
men? But can love between men ever be "simple" when it corresponds
historically with the consolidation of power between them and their dom-
ination over others? To consider such questions seriously is to risk pro-
moting the belief that taking pleasure in these photographs requires a
certain ignorance about the reality they picture.

But what of the relationships that other gay men have sustained to
such photographs? What of collectors—men in their sixties and seven-
ties—who came of age not only before AIDS established circumstances
in which the gay predisposition to morbidity assumed disastrous new
meanings, but before the inception of the mass movement for gay sexual
freedom and civil rights made it possible for gay men to live more openly?

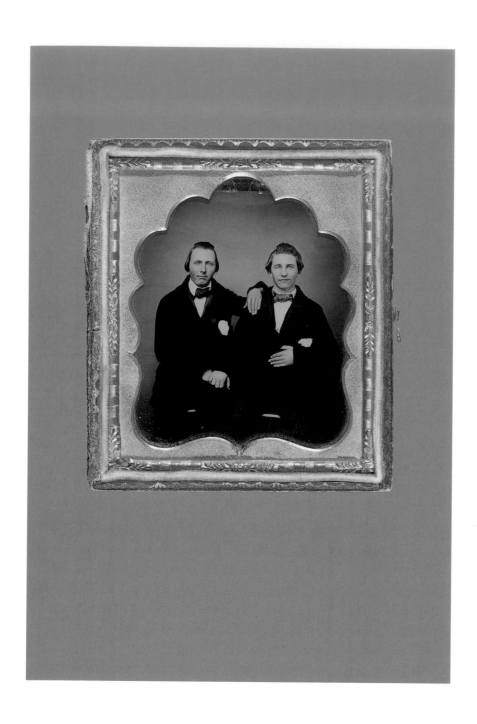

PHOTOGRAPHER UNKNOWN, SUBJECTS UNKNOWN, 1/6-PLATE AMBROTYPE (3⅝ × 3⅛"), C. 1865

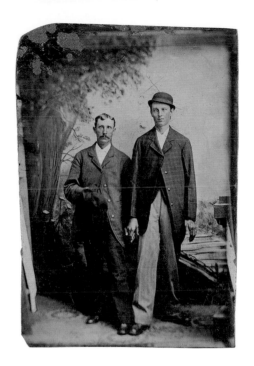

PHOTOGRAPHER UNKNOWN, SUBJECTS UNKNOWN, TINTYPE (3½ × 2⅜"), C. 1880

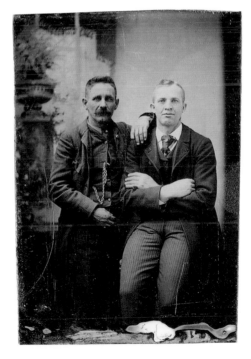

PHOTOGRAPHER UNKNOWN, SUBJECTS UNKNOWN, TINTYPE (3½ × 2⅜"), C. 1890

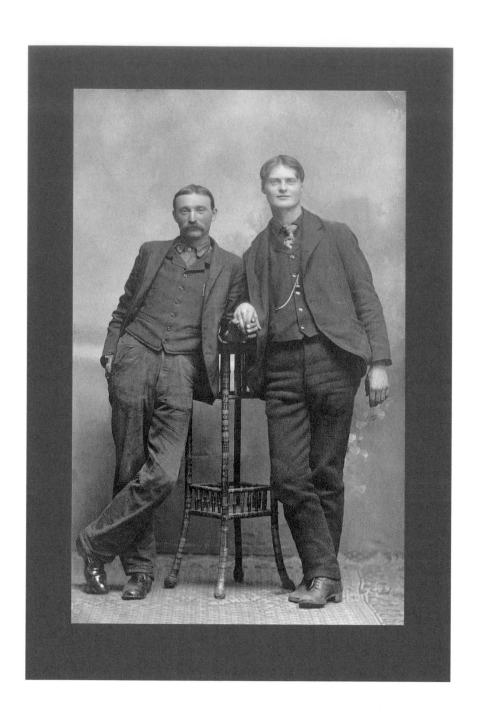

PHOTOGRAPHER UNKNOWN, SUBJECTS UNKNOWN, GELATIN SILVER PRINT, REAL PHOTO POSTCARD (5½ × 3½"), C. 1915

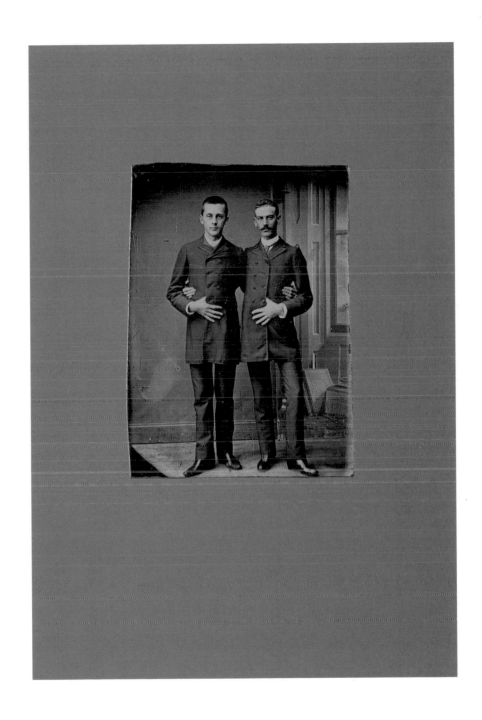

PHOTOGRAPHER UNKNOWN, SUBJECTS UNKNOWN, TINTYPE (3^1/$_4$ × 3″), C. 1880

Under those conditions, such men would have been drawn to these photographs as rare historical emblems of their desire. When representations of same-sex love are forbidden, images of men together, which the guardians of mainstream propriety consider innocuous enough to leave unregulated, become cherished objects of desire. This happens through a more or less conscious act of willful misinterpretation. As an adolescent, I remember satisfying my yearning for representations of same-sex sexuality, of male flesh against male flesh, by looking at the photographs of swimmers that illustrated the "Junior Lifesaving" manuals of the American Red Cross. In retrospect, that willful misuse of vernacular imagery had about it an unmistakable charm, as did the accompanying projection of erotic scenarios onto these purely functional stagings of seminaked men in distress being rescued by others.

Today we can swim in seas of homoerotica and X-rated porn. It should not be taken as a detraction from the pleasures of porn to underscore the guilelessness and ingenuity with which image-starved gay men and lesbians once perused everyday representations for sexual excitement; nor to admit to mourning the passage of such creative strategies for (homo)sexual survival as one of the costs we have had to pay for replacing gay subcultural ingenuity with gay culture, *tout court*. [7] There are, of course, other related trade-offs in which one thing is lost at the price of another being gained. Ultimately, this book provides evidence of a parallel trade-off that results from the historical transformation of the social meaning of same-sex affection from a nineteenth-century tradition of romantic friendship and comradely love to the considerably more recent, modern category of homosexuality. Among the casualties of this reconceptualization of same-sex affection was the more fluid affection that characterized romantic friendship and comradely love, and its physical expression among men who posed for photographers holding hands, entwining limbs, or resting in the shelter of each other's accommodating bodies, innocent of the suspicion that such behavior would later arouse. What was gained would take the better part of half a century to crystallize: the awakening of gay men and lesbians to the political nature of their modern oppression, which then led to the making, in the historian John D'Emilio's phrase, of a "homosexual minority in the United States." [8]

Tragedy, past and present, can provoke acts of defiance. Symbolic defiance is implicit in the act of historical reclamation and brings pleasure and persistence to the search for evidence of a past, even if it includes the debris of lives wrecked by antiquated injunctions or disfigured by more modern technologies for regulating desire. Resistance compels the queer historian to unearth precious traces of that past and to disseminate them in the form of previously untold stories of men and women, some of whom succeeded as others failed to live with and act on their forbidden love. Through such acts of recuperation, the queer historian helps to ensure the continued availability of that past as a source of validation and connection for similarly isolated individuals in the future.

The fact that the photographs in this book can ultimately only perpetuate uncertainty regarding precisely what they picture in no way detracts from the significance of their recovery and collection. From a queer perspective, this self-imposed horizon of historical knowledge has a salutary effect, inasmuch as it rejects the hubris that so often motivates more elaborately legitimated attempts at historical reclamation.[9] Nor should the importance of this modest salvage operation be denied on the basis of its speculative (and therefore depreciated) historical method. Central to that speculative method is the self-validating faith in the potential of private desire to lead to the disclosure of public truth.

★   ★   ★

It was as recently as in 1975 that feminist historian Caroll Smith-Rosenberg focused attention for the first time on the evidence of "intimate friendships" between nineteenth-century women, applying to their letters and diaries the kind of rigorous analysis required to understand such documents. One of Smith-Rosenberg's purposes—and achievements— was to interpret romantic friendship within the context of its Victorian social circumstances, rather than from a twentieth-century psychosocial perspective, which would have distorted its meaning. Rather than proceed from our "dichotomized universe of deviance and normality, genitality and platonic love," concepts that would have been "alien to the emotions and attitudes of the nineteenth century," Smith-Rosenberg analyzed these passionate attachments within the context of the segregated male and female social spheres that she attributed to "rigid gender-role differentiation within the family and within society as a whole."[10] During Alexis de Tocqueville's American sojourn of 1830–31, he had noticed the demarcation of such gender-specific social spheres. "In America," he observed, "more than anywhere else in the world, care has been taken to constantly trace clearly the distinct spheres of action of the two sexes and both are required to keep in step, but along paths that are never the same."[11] To Smith-Rosenberg's suggestive understanding of romantic friendship as a function, in part, of segregated male and female social worlds, other historians would add allusions to the rise of wage labor, mass transience, and the concomitant pressure on men to live and work apart from women and families in situations that ranged from burgeoning factory towns and cities to the American frontier.[12] According to Smith-Rosenberg, the sanction granted romantic same-sex friendship endowed Victorian women with greater freedom to traverse the affective spectrum between "committed heterosexuality" and "uncompromising homosexuality" than would be available in the following century.[13]

The journal of Albert Dodd, a Yale student during the late 1830s, provides evidence of the kind of passionate attachments that arose between privileged young men within the university's all-male preserve. On February 4, 1837, Dodd wrote about his love for a young man named John: "I regard, I esteem, I love him more than all the rest," he claimed, thereby alluding to others—male and female, as it happens—who also had attracted his devoted attention.[14] Attempting to sort out his feelings, Dodd added, "it is not friendship merely which I feel for him, or it is friendship of the strongest kind. It is a heart-felt, a manly, a pure, deep, and fervent love." That this intense young man regarded such heart-felt, manly love as "pure" strikes the "dichotomized" twentieth-century observer as noteworthy; not so for Dodd's contemporaries. Nor was his invocation of purity necessarily made in guilty denial of a deeply rooted culpability. Dodd's evaluation of his fervent attachment to John reflects the acceptance, if not the prestige, then accorded such relationships as a result of the tradition of romantic friendship, which dated back to the latter half of the eighteenth century. Dodd's feelings for John are merely the unbridled (if hackneyed) expression of emotions that Whitman redeemed as upright in *Democratic Vistas*, where they materialize as "threads of manly friendship, fond and loving, pure and sweet, strong and lifelong."[15]

Rare though its survival is, Dodd's journal is hardly unique in providing evidence of the scope and intensity of the intimate ties that were acceptable among nineteenth-century Americans. Rotundo has documented a host of other relationships, including those between a youthful Daniel Webster and Hervey Bingham, James Blake and Wyck Vanderhoef, the artist John Lambert and Sergeant Kendall, as well as the youthful infatuation of Ralph Waldo Emerson for Martin Gay. Such romantic same-sex feelings remind us, Rotundo writes, that "in spite of separate

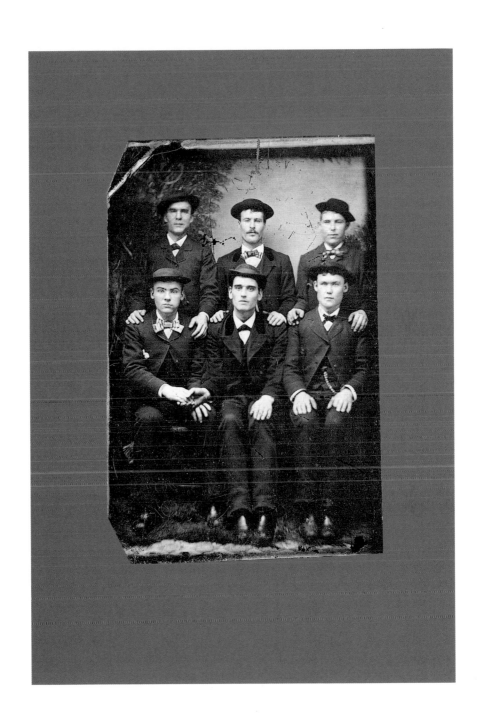

PHOTOGRAPHER UNKNOWN, SUBJECTS UNKNOWN, TINTYPE (3¾ × 2⅛″), C. 1875

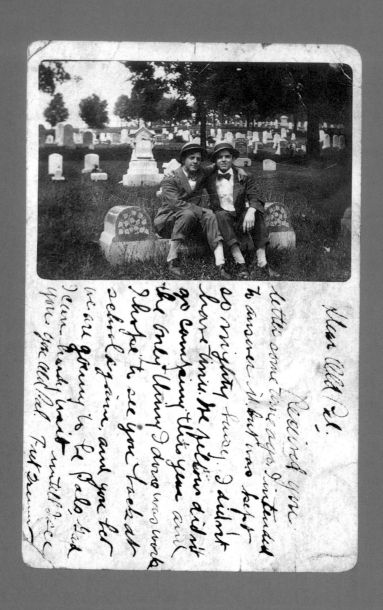

PHOTOGRAPHER UNKNOWN, SUBJECTS UNKNOWN, GELATIN SILVER PRINT, REAL PHOTO POSTCARD (5½ × 3½"),
C. 1915. INSCRIPTION READS: "DEAR OLD PAL,/RECEIVED YOUR/LETTER SOME TIME AGO. I INTENDED/TO ANSWER IT
BUT WAS KEPT/SO MIGHTY BUSY I DIDN'T/HAVE TIME. WE FELLOWS DIDN'T/GO CAMPING THIS YEAR AND/THE ONLY
THING I DONE WAS WORK./I HOPE TO SEE YOU BACK AT/SCHOOL AGAIN AND YOU BET WE ARE GOING TO BE PALS.
GAD/I CAN HARDLY WAIT UNTIL I SEE/YOU. YOUR OLD PAL [ILLEG.]"

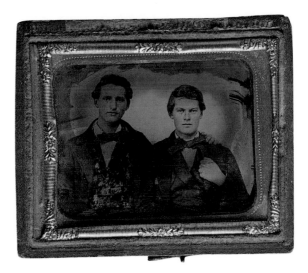

spheres and separate male and female cultures, men and women of the nineteenth century continued to share basic emotional capacities, like the capacity for forming intimate same-sex bonds." In the twentieth century, he notes, the ardor that had developed between such young men "would seem unusual outside of gay circles."[16] But in the nineteenth century, it was not considered unusual for letters such as those between Webster and Bingham to open with such salutations as "Lovely Boy" or "Dearly Beloved"; to be peppered with such terms of endearment as "my Hervey" and "my dearest J.H.B."; and to end, affectionately, "I am, dear Hervey, your Daniel Webster," or "Accept all the tenderness I have, D. Webster."[17]

Nor did it deviate from mainstream social convention for Emerson to compose a private love poem for Gay, although he did feel obliged to mask the latter's identity by replacing "Martin" with "Malcomb"—perhaps out of deference to the latter's privacy.

> *Malcomb, I love thee more than women love*
> *And pure and warm and equal is the feeling*
> *Which binds as one our destinies forever*
> *But there are seasons in the change of times*
> *When strong excitement kindles up the light*
> *of ancient memories.*[18]

Smith-Rosenberg's recognition of the ease with which nineteenth-century American women directed their affections to members of the same sex corresponded with the historical realization that the category of the homosexual is a late-nineteenth-century European invention. By the late 1980s, when social historians of masculinity started to focus attention on the documentary evidence of fervent ties between American men, they made a point of acknowledging Smith-Rosenberg's cautionary distinction between Victorian and modern perspectives on passionate friendship. They also noted that the absence of a word, and therefore of a concept, for the homosexual had a distinctly beneficial effect on such affectionate same-sex relations. Rotundo expressed an increasingly popular understanding among his colleagues when he observed in 1989: "The single most revealing fact about middle-class attitudes toward homosexuality in the 1800s is that there was no such term."[19] Much has been made of this "constructionist" view of homosexuality as a historically contingent term—a modern classification for human beings that only gradually

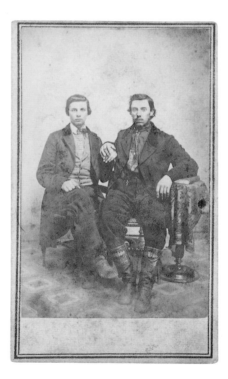

PHOTOGRAPHER UNKNOWN, SUBJECTS UNKNOWN, CARTE DE VISITE (4 × 2½"),
C. 1863. 3-CENT INTERNAL REVENUE PROPRIETARY STAMP ON VERSO

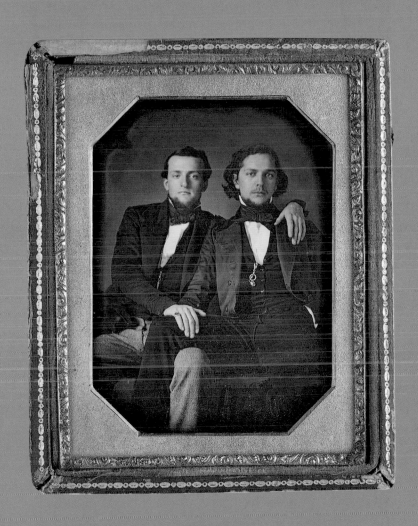

PHOTOGRAPHER UNKNOWN, SUBJECTS UNKNOWN, ¼-PLATE DAGUERREOTYPE (4³/₄ × 3⁷/₈"), C. 1845–50

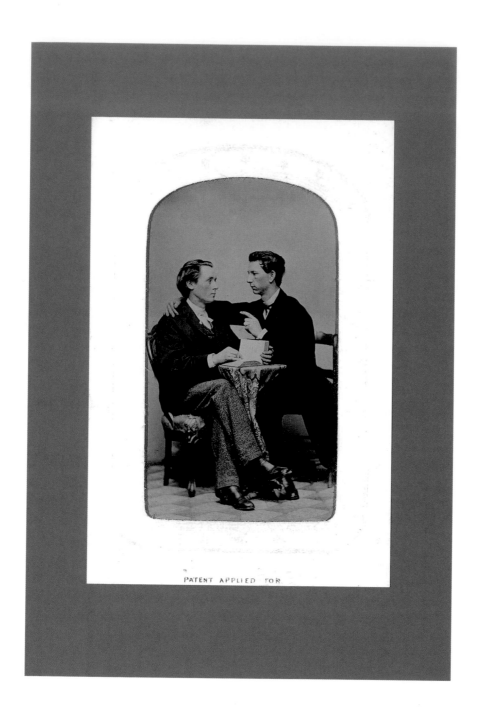

PHOTOGRAPHER UNKNOWN, SUBJECTS UNKNOWN, TINTYPE IN PAPER SLEEVE (OVERALL: 3³/₄ × 2¹/₂″), C. 1875

acquired its name and meaning at the confluence of medical, psychological, and criminological European discourses during the last quarter of the nineteenth century.[20]

Yet it is one thing to acknowledge the lack of a word and a concept for homosexuality, and quite another to understand what that implies for heterosexuality—a word and a concept that also did not exist during the heyday of romantic same-sex friendship. Heterosexual historians (that is, historians who invariably "come out" as straight by acknowledging at the beginning of their published works the untiring patience and support of their spouses and children) have been content to find in the absence of the category *homosexual* reason to presume the heterosexuality of nineteenth-century American men who fervently loved other men.[21] In this way, the straight historian's argument mirrors homophobically the insistence among gay observers who heedlessly presume that in nineteenth-century photographs of anonymous, affectionate men they have discovered incontrovertible evidence of the past they yearn to find.

★   ★   ★

Social historians have observed that the romantic effusions that men expressed for each other revealed a greater diversity of acceptable masculine behavior than one might expect during the independent-minded and supremely competitive Jacksonian era. Rotundo notes, however, that romantic friendships between men differed in one significant respect from similarly passionate ties between women, inasmuch as they were limited to playing a "vital role" during the transitional period of youth. Despite Whitman's claims to the contrary, these were not the "life-long" bonds that women enjoyed.[22] Yet there is ample documentation to prove that romantic friendships between men did indeed endure well past youth, although marriage did become an impediment. For example, the effusive language of romantic friendship dominated correspondence between American and British abolitionists. Thirty years of challenging, sometimes dangerous, cooperative work at advancing antislavery reform did not dull the Unitarian minister Samuel Joseph May's proclamations of fervent love for William Lloyd Garrison. In an attempt to alleviate the burden that the abolitionist struggle was imposing on Garrison, in 1860 May proposed: "If I were a wealthy man I would take you in my arms, or on the wings of wind or steam—and bear you off to Egypt, Palestine,

Greece, Italy, etc. etc.—and you might be taken out of your cares." Photography also played a supporting role in marking and extending the life of such tender ties. As late as 1867 Garrison kept a photograph of May in his study.[23]

At the age of forty-four, the British abolitionist Charles Stuart established "an enduring bond" with the fifteen-year-old American Theodore Dwight Weld. Their friendship was marked by rapturous correspondence: "Adieu, my Theodore, dearer than any ties of blood could make you," Stuart wrote after visiting with Weld in 1828. "My soul pants once more to embrace you." And if Weld's marriage to Angelina Grimké effectively terminated the "indivisible existence" that hitherto had marked the two men's lives, the pain of their separation persisted long afterward. "His absence almost seems like the subtraction of a portion of my being," Weld wrote in 1837. Long after their split, in 1855, Stuart still affirmed: "I love him—I could *almost* wish myself accursed from Christ, for him." This was a rather remarkable assertion, especially given the fact that the abolitionists' love for one another was, according to the historian Donald Yacavone, modeled after *agape*, the fraternal love that dominated the Early Christian Church, which was itself inspired by Christ's love for mankind, and the twelve apostles' love for Christ and one another.[24]

At different times throughout the nineteenth century, and for different reasons, classically educated American and British men were also inclined to exalt their romantic same-sex attachments with ennobling, and chastening, references to David and Jonathan, Plato and Aristotle, Damon and Pythias, Achilles and Patroclus. Addressing the later nineteenth-century tendency to hellenize references to same-sex love by advocates of aestheticism and/or by homosexuals, the historian Peter Gay has noted: "To assimilate modern homosexual affairs to the exalted classical heritage was to borrow from its dignity, to claim a kind of historic rightness. The device was transparent, but no less popular for all that."[25] At the height of the Victorian cult of friendship, passionate same-sex affection between social equals was viewed as pure, in contrast to its complement between men and women. Notwithstanding the religious sanctification of marriage, the love of husband and wife could not aspire to the immaculate spirituality of same-sex romance, in part because of the instrumentality implicit in procreative sex, and in part because such love was tainted by lustful cravings that Victorians found too easily assimilable to the instinctual drives of the animal kingdom.

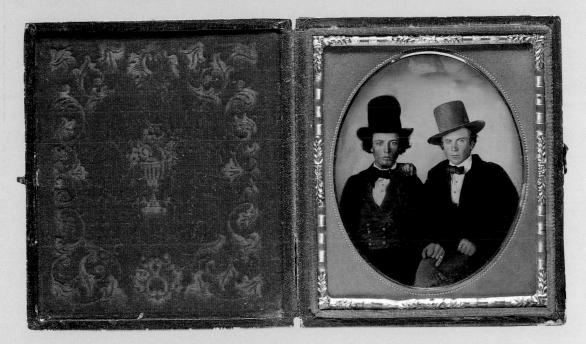

PHOTOGRAPHER UNKNOWN, SUBJECTS UNKNOWN, ⅙-PLATE AMBROTYPE (3¾ × 3¼″), C. 1855–60.

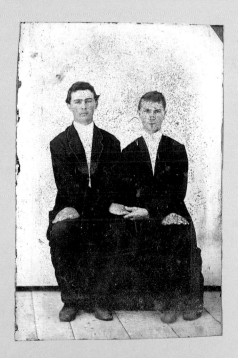

PHOTOGRAPHER UNKNOWN, SUBJECTS UNKNOWN, TINTYPE (3¾ × 2½″), C. 1870

Same-sex romantic friendship could be cherished as pure despite the fact that fervent emotion could, and often did, correspond with physical intimacy. After Albert Dodd found a responsive object of his affections in Anthony Halsey (his entreaties to John fell on deaf ears), he noted the ensuing raptures in his journal: "Often too he shared my pillow—or I his, and how sweet to sleep with him, to hold his beloved form in my embrace, to have his arms about my neck, to imprint upon his face sweet kisses!" As Smith-Rosenberg foresaw, the twentieth-century inclination to classify human intimacies in terms of either a normal or a deviant sexuality has made it difficult for historians to come to terms with the meaning of more fluid affections. The tenacity of this either/or reflex is reflected in a statement such as "the embraces and kisses one friend bestowed on the other remained mere epistolary effusions"[26]; or in the assertion that nineteenth-century American men who commonly shared beds did so throughout their lives, "without homoerotic desire or the suspicion of homoerotic intent."[27] Even if one were to grant the likelihood of such a claim in the majority of cases, it would hardly preclude the possibility that there were also other men who participated in such sleeping arrangements, or who engaged in such commonplace embraces, who did so with homoerotic desire and even "homoerotic intent" (whatever that is). The naturalized projection onto the past of our dichotomized view of intimacy also surfaces in the heedless deployment of the word "innocent" to describe the emotions and activities of romantic friends, in and out of bed, thereby implying the guilt of more knowing relations.[28]

In exploring the limits of the physical intimacies that took place within the historical context of socially sanctioned same-sex love, a measure of elasticity has been adopted. This seems merely prudent, considering how impossible it is to ascertain precisely what did go on in bed between Dodd and Halsey, between Daniel Webster and Hervey Bingham, or between the young storekeeper from New Salem, Illinois, named Joshua Speed, who shared his bed with Abraham Lincoln—let alone what went on in beds and on city streets between other men (and women) who, like the amorous couples in these photographs, never did document their sexual activities in words that have survived.[29] What constellation of mitigating social circumstances accompanied this Victorian sanction? And how might those circumstances affect the meaning of passionate friendships between men and of the photographic practice that commemorated such close ties?

★　　★　　★

The readiness with which a likeness may be obtained, the
truthfulness of the image, and the smallness of cost, render
it the current pledge of friendship.
　　　　　　　　　　　—HORACE GREELEY, 1853

Many of the most striking photographs of affectionate
pairs of men date from the second third of the nineteenth century—a
time when American life was decidedly not marked by the kind of social
cohesion and harmony that these photographs suggest, but by division,
dislocation, fear, and mistrust. Approximately seven years before the
introduction of photography to the United States, the isolation of the
American man had already attracted Tocqueville's attention. "Not only
does democracy make every man forget his ancestors, but it hides his
descendants and separates his contemporaries from him; it throws him
back forever upon himself alone and threatens in the end to confine him
entirely within the solitude of his heart."[30] But it was not simply the
republican system of American government that perpetuated the confinement of the American man "within the solitude of his heart." From
the period of Tocqueville's sojourn and, increasingly, until well after the
Civil War, social life in the United States underwent a series of profound
transformations. These changes undermined the artisanal mode of production and trade that arguably had lent a measure of social cohesion
and equilibrium to life and work from the mid-eighteenth century into
the early 1800s. The artisanal way of life was characterized by the small-
scale manufacture of goods for home use and trade in a local market. The
artisan—honored by Thomas Jefferson as the "yeomanry of the city"—
might work with the aid of one or two journeymen, and a young
apprentice who lived under his roof and to whom he imparted the "art
and mystery" of his craft. Artisans worked in small teams as tailors, shoe-
makers, barrel makers, tanners, blacksmiths, printers, hatters, cabinetmakers,
and carriage makers, with the master overseeing every aspect of the business from ordering materials and keeping the books to working along
with and supervising employees and selling completed goods to local
clients in face-to-face transactions.

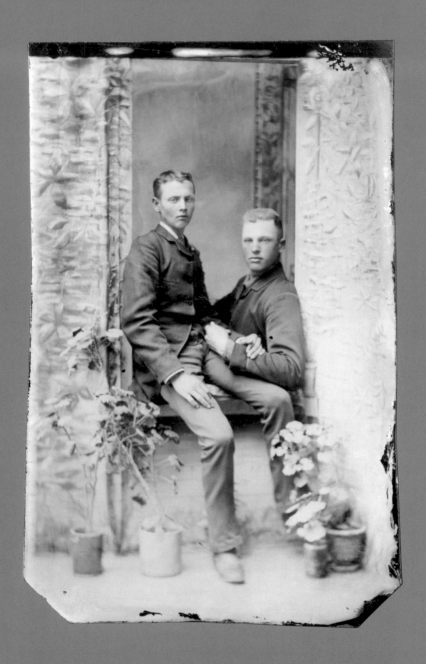

PHOTOGRAPHER UNKNOWN, SUBJECTS UNKNOWN, TINTYPE (6¾ × 4″), C. 1870

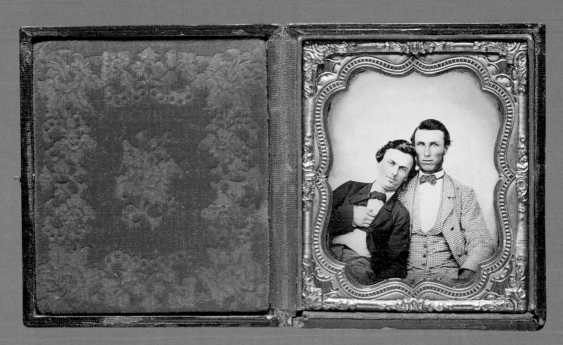

PHOTOGRAPHER UNKNOWN, SUBJECTS UNKNOWN, 1/6-PLATE AMBROTYPE (3¾ × 3¼″), C. 1865

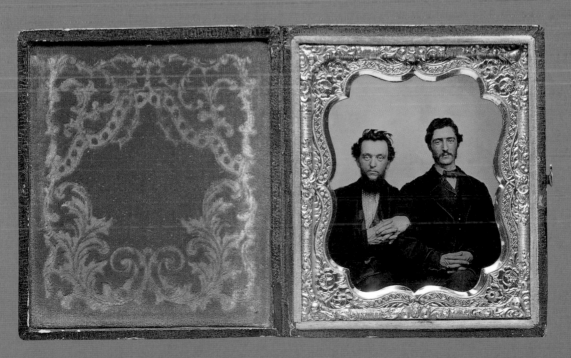

PHOTOGRAPHER UNKNOWN, SUBJECTS UNKNOWN, TINTYPE (3¾ × 3¼″), C. 1865

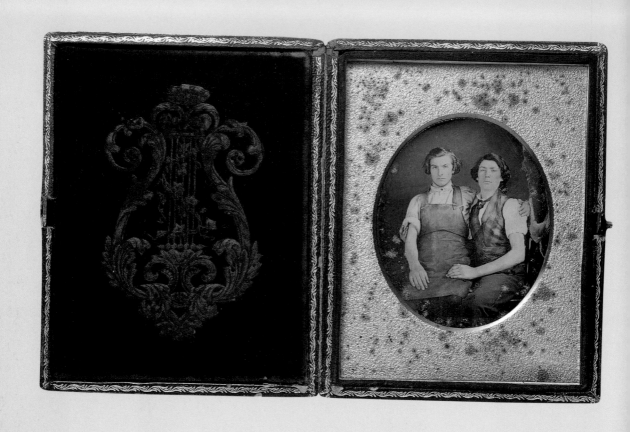

PHOTOGRAPHER UNKNOWN, SUBJECTS UNKNOWN, ¼-PLATE DAGUERREOTYPE (4¾ × 3¾ "), C. 1850

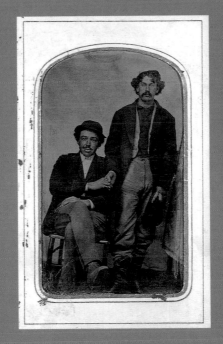

PHOTOGRAPHER UNKNOWN, SUBJECTS UNKNOWN, TINTYPE IN PAPER SLEEVE (OVERALL: 4 × 2¹/₂″), C. 1865–70

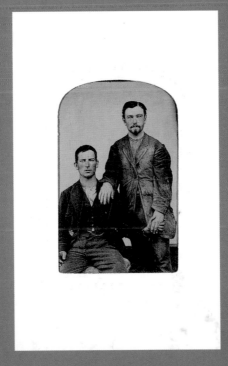

PHOTOGRAPHER UNKNOWN, SUBJECTS UNKNOWN, TINTYPE IN PAPER SLEEVE (OVERALL: 3⁷/₈ × 2³/₈″), C. 1865

Henry Wright Clark, a hatter from Newark and a future abolitionist, substantiated the romanticized view of the artisanal way of life when he described his pleasure in work. "I felt real satisfaction in being able to make a hat," he wrote, "because I loved to contemplate the work, and because I felt pleasure in carrying through the various stages."[31] But the mid-nineteenth-century revolution in the quality and quantity of production, in the way products were sold and markets defined, necessarily changed the way people thought of themselves and experienced their relations with others. And in the vast majority of cases, this revolutionary process eliminated from work the contemplative satisfaction that Clark describes, as well as the friendly banter that took place among workers engaged in such activities.

The roots of this transformation of the social relations of production and trade can be traced to the late eighteenth century, to the construction of roads and turn-

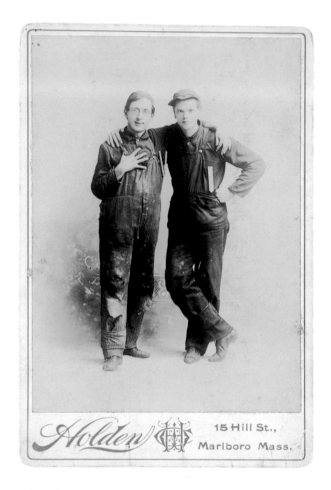

CHARLES W. HOLDEN [?], SUBJECTS UNKNOWN, CABINET CARD (6½ × 4¼"), C. 1900–10. IMPRINT READS: "HOLDEN 15 HILL ST., /MARLBORO MASS."

pikes that foreshadowed the revolution in American transportation culminating in 1825 with the completion of the Erie Canal. Even before the introduction of railways during the 1830s, such improvements in transportation facilitated the spread of protoindustrial innovations in production and trade that historians have identified with the telltale structures of commercial capitalism. The displacement of barter by the use of money and the introduction of wage labor, rudimentary task differentiation, and "outwork" (the replacement of skilled labor by less skilled, often female workers who labored on piecework in the seclusion of their homes) eroded local pockets of craft independence.

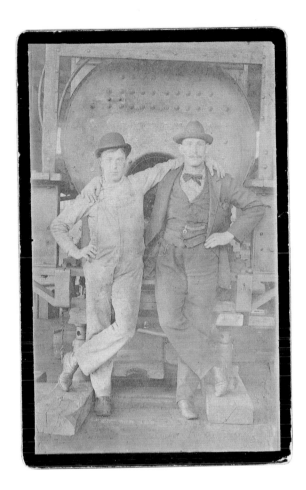

PHOTOGRAPHER UNKNOWN, SUBJECTS UNKNOWN, CABINET CARD (OVERALL: 8⁷/₁₆ × 5¹/₄"), C. 1890–1900. INSCRIPTION ON VERSO READS: "THEODOR LEFT L.N. GRONER RIGHT TAKING IN BELLWOOD SHOPS BACK OF NO. 1 ENGINE"

The artisanal way of life was undermined by the increased competition that resulted from large-scale production of ready-made goods intended for sale in the more distant markets, which improved transportation brought within affordable reach. To be sure, craft-based production did persist (though mostly in the creation of goods for the well-to-do), but even within these smaller-scale economies the conditions of production changed. For example, one historian notes: "In two great bursts of fifteen years each following the [economic] downturns of 1819–21 and 1837–43, most handicraft workshops shed their easy ambiance." In the printing trades, where the skilled labor of typesetters had been essential, "sweated labor" became necessary to increase production and decrease costs. During this protoindustrial period, workers continued to use hand tools in small shops and homes, but they did so to execute tasks that were increasingly simplified by the division of labor. The introduction of task differentiation transformed the production of ready-made clothing (of "coarse wear" for use by the military, southern slaves, and western farmers) into a "bastion of sweated labor." The relentlessly competitive system of sweated labor resulted in a "tangle of brutally exploitative relations not only between employer and employee but between employees themselves."[32] There could be few, if any, constraints on the exploitative relations that employers maintained with workers in Jacksonian America. This was, after all, a period that witnessed the crystallization of an ideological figure who would prove as durable as he was forceful in his own day: the self-made American man, for whom unbridled competitiveness, individualism, and progress were unquestioned virtues.

By the middle of the nineteenth century, but especially after the Civil War, mechanization accelerated the destruction of the family- and craft-centered way of life, even as it helped to further the separation of home and work. With the circular logic of a closed system, job simplification "made it possible to use machines and the machines intensified the division of labor."[33] Whereas commercial capitalism in its preindustrial phase had reorganized production socially, industrialized capitalism reorganized it technically through the mechanization of human labor. Industrial production then required the physical proximity of workers with machinery in a clearly delineated workplace: the factory. With the construction of factories, inland towns and coastal cities came to reflect physically, and to perpetuate in the process, the further fragmentation of American social life along the lines of class, ethnicity, and race. And while industrialization made it possible for some people to work close to home and family, it did nothing to diminish the enormous numbers of unskilled Americans who migrated from one town or city to another in search of jobs that lasted only as long as the vagaries of market conditions allowed, or who fled such conditions altogether in the hopes of establishing more satisfying lives on the American frontier.

Nor did industrialization do anything to alleviate the isolation of workers who did find jobs. Successive waves of commercial and industrial innovation transformed the workplace into the setting for another distinctly modern invention, yet another form of solitude: alienation. This estrangement from one's creative capacities, from the product of one's own labor, and from other people represents the polar opposite of Henry Wright Clark's idyllic account of the contemplative satisfaction he experienced in making hats. The understanding of alienation as the product of the capitalist division of labor, of the mechanized acceleration of ever more fragmentary, repetitive, and monotonous tasks, and of the leveling of everyday life as a result of commodification finds support not only in the writings of Karl Marx but, ironically, in a fragment from one of three mid-nineteenth-century essays on photography that Oliver Wendell Holmes published in the *Atlantic Monthly*. In "Doings of the Sunbeam" (1863), the Brahmin poet and physician takes the reader on a brief behind-the-scenes tour of one of the larger purveyors of photography at the time, "Messers. E. & H. T. Anthony, in Broadway, New York." There, he describes the on-the-job activities of one dispirited worker in terms that Marx might have seized on. "The workmen in large establishments,"

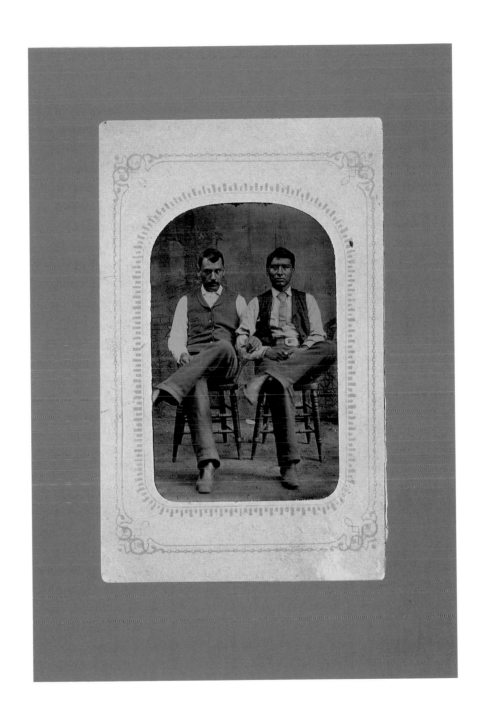

PHOTOGRAPHER UNKNOWN, SUBJECTS UNKNOWN, TINTYPE IN PAPER SLEEVE (OVERALL: 3¹/₄ × 2¹/₄″), C. 1885

reports Holmes, "where labor is greatly subdivided, become wonderfully adroit in doing a fraction of something."

A young person who mounts photographs on cards all day long confessed to having never, or almost never, seen a negative developed, though standing at the time within a few feet of the dark closet where the process was going on all day long. One forlorn individual will perhaps pass his days in a single work of cleaning the glass plates for negatives. Almost at his elbow is a toning bath, but he would think it a good joke, if you asked him whether a picture has lain long enough in the solution of gold or hyposulphite.[34]

The photo historian Alan Trachtenberg has addressed the social signifi-cance of Holmes's account from a neo-Marxist perspective, observing that as a commercial enterprise, photography functioned under the dis-tinct social relations of industrial capitalism, which in their way had helped to shape photographic practice. Specifically, Trachtenberg relates Holmes's description of the alienated employee to the "growing numbers of lonely persons who found in photography some forlorn hope of alle-viating isolation through the exchange of images."[35] It was precisely such trade in photographic portraits that the editor-journalist Horace Greeley had pronounced the "current pledge of friendship" in 1853, when he reported on "art and industry" at New York's Crystal Palace exhibition.[36]

Two years before the publication of Holmes's article, in 1861, the photographer Marcus Aurelius Root singled out the sentimental role of the keepsake as one of two principal social functions for portrait photog-raphy. Through the agency of photography, Root observed, "our loved ones, dead or distant; our friends and acquaintances, however far removed, are retained within daily and hourly vision." Root then alluded to the broader social context in which this flourishing trade could acquire the material-ist significance that Trachtenberg assigned to it retroactively. "In this com-petitious and selfish world of ours," Root maintained, "whatever tends to vivify and strengthen the social feelings should be hailed as a benediction."[37]

It was unquestionably this private, sentimental function of portrait photography that appealed to the many pairs of men who commemorat-ed intimate friendships by posing together so affectionately before the camera. The survival of thousands of these photographs attests to the prevalence of such intimate ties between men; this despite—or perhaps because of—the isolation and rootlessness that were such prominent

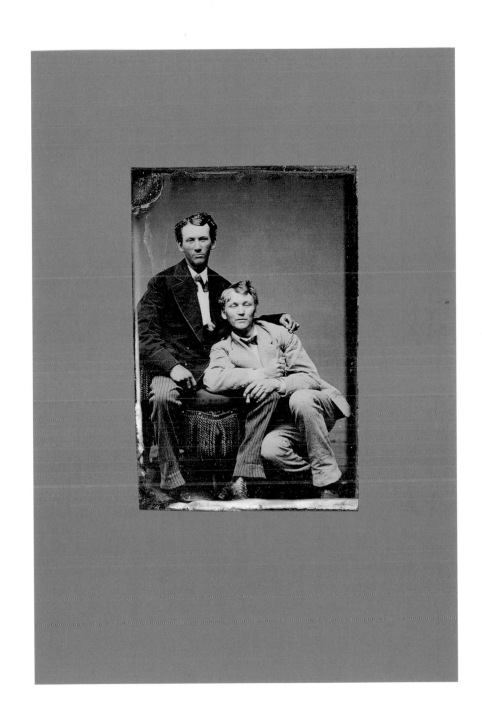

PHOTOGRAPHER UNKNOWN, SUBJECTS UNKNOWN, TINTYPE (3$^1/_2$ × 2$^3/_8$"), C. 1875

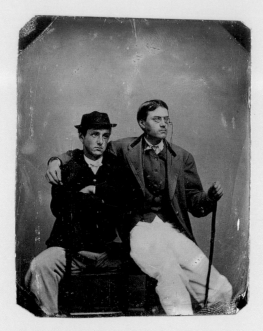

PHOTOGRAPHER UNKNOWN, SUBJECTS UNKNOWN, TINTYPE (3$\frac{1}{8}$ × 2$\frac{1}{2}$″), C. 1875–80

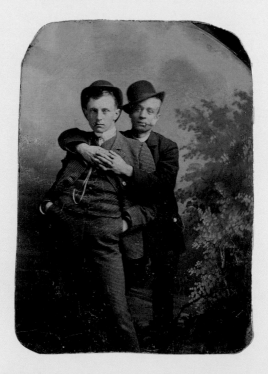

PHOTOGRAPHER UNKNOWN, SUBJECTS UNKNOWN, TINTYPE (3$\frac{5}{8}$ × 2$\frac{1}{2}$″), C. 1885

74

aspects of nineteenth-century American society. The pervasive mass transience that defined life for many nineteenth-century Americans contributed to the allure of intimate friendship, in part as a consequence of its being rare and difficult to maintain.[38] At first glance, the evidence of a cult of friendship may appear to contradict the image of the nineteenth-century American man as imprisoned within his solitude—whether as a product of his successful adaptation to the Jacksonian creed of independence, competition, and the single-minded pursuit of prosperity, or because of the dehumanizing effects of industrial capitalism. Given further consideration, it is not hard to see that in the harshness of those "competitious and selfish times" friendship, and the sentimental practices of correspon-

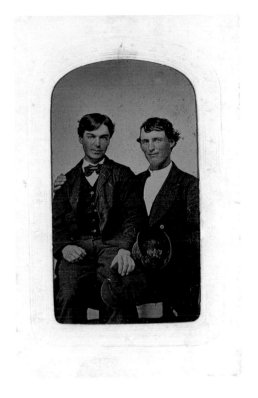

dence and commemorative portrait photography, would be cherished by Americans who could turn to them to counter the human cost of social developments that otherwise effected estrangement. Not only did photographs of intimate friends make it possible to keep the image of an absent loved one close at hand, they provided evidence of comfort and love in the midst of widespread social disruption and human disconnection.

★   ★   ★

The comfort and consolation that nineteenth-century men could find in friendship and its photographic complement would be mirrored, admittedly with a difference, in the mid-twentieth century by gay men who were among the first to find value in surviving photographs of affectionately posed pairs of men. For while attention has been lavished on the documentary evidence of romantic friendship, none has been paid to its remarkable visual counterpart in which men posed together in the somewhat less than private circumstances of commercial photography studios holding hands, hugging, laying a hand on a friend's shoulder or resting it along his thigh, sitting on his lap, or reclining within the shelter of his body. The vast majority of these photographs were cultural cast-offs, having been dispersed following the sitters' deaths. As anonymous photographs of anonymous men, they have been of interest neither to museum curators nor to big-time photography collectors who more readily respond to authenticated works by celebrated artists or to imagery of regional and historical interest—a category that has decidedly not included historic representations of same-sex love. Thus, it is among the stalls of flea markets, photo fairs, and modest antique shops that these objects resurface initially, to be found and rescued from oblivion by enthusiastic devotees—most of them gay.

It is one thing to describe what such photographs represent (for the gay man who collects them with such avidity), quite another to claim to know with any degree of historical precision what it is that they depict.

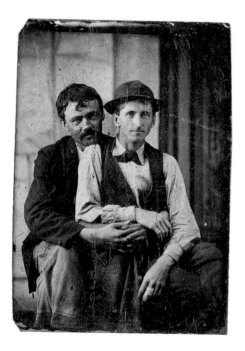

PHOTOGRAPHER UNKNOWN, SUBJECTS UNKNOWN, TINTYPE (3¼ × 2½″), 1870

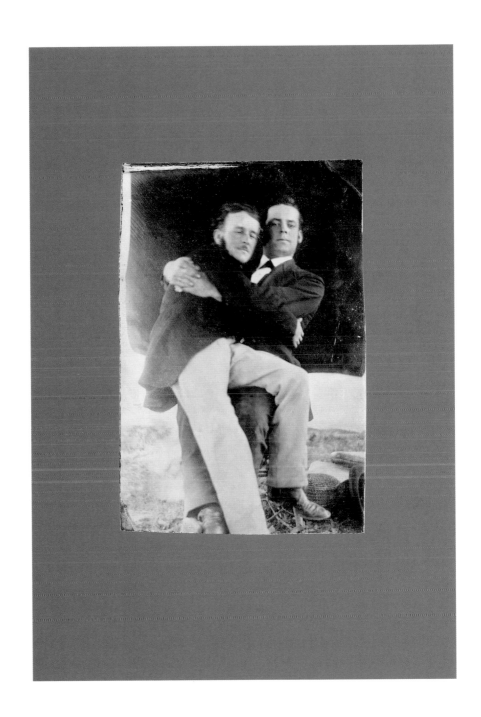

PHOTOGRAPHER UNKNOWN, SUBJECTS UNKNOWN, TINTYPE (3⁷/₈ × 2⁵/₈"), C. 1900

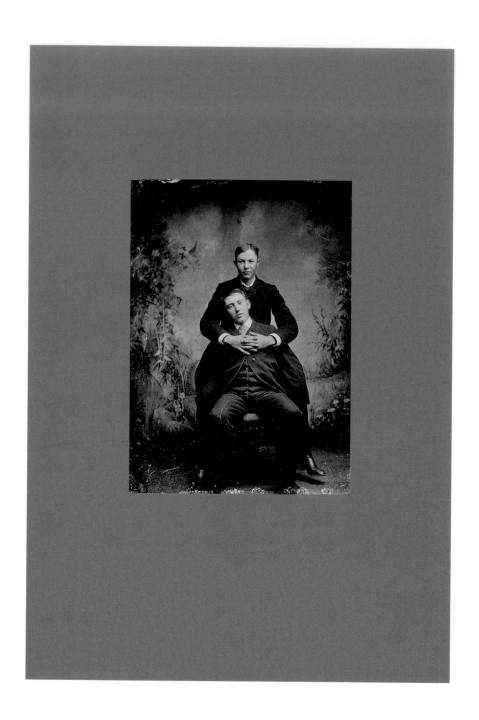

PHOTOGRAPHER UNKNOWN, SUBJECTS UNKNOWN, TINTYPE (3¼ × 2⅜"), C. 1875

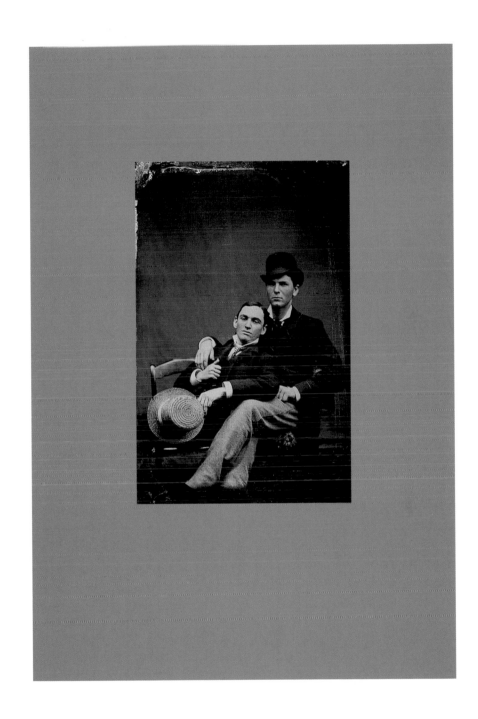

PHOTOGRAPHER UNKNOWN, SUBJECTS UNKNOWN, TINTYPE (3¹/₂ × 2¹/₄"), C. 1875–80

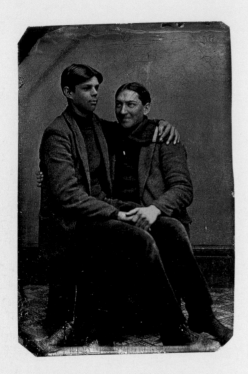

PHOTOGRAPHER UNKNOWN, SUBJECTS UNKNOWN,
TINTYPE (3½ × 2¼″), C. 1875

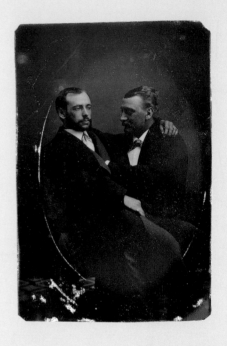

PHOTOGRAPHER UNKNOWN, SUBJECTS UNKNOWN,
TINTYPE (3⅛ × 2″), C. 1880

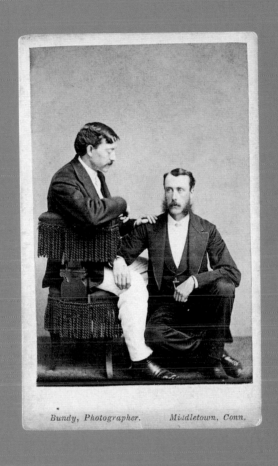

Bundy, Photographer.   Middletown, Conn.

JOSEPH K. BUNDY, SUBJECTS UNKNOWN, CARTE DE VISTE (4 × 2½"), C. 1860.
IMPRINT READS: "BUNDY, PHOTOGRAPHER MIDDLETOWN, CONN."

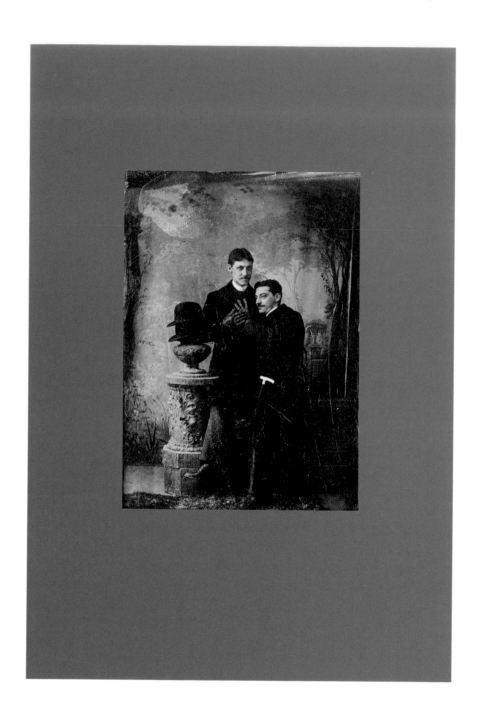

PHOTOGRAPHER UNKNOWN, SUBJECTS UNKNOWN, TINTYPE (3^1/$_2$ × 2^1/$_2$″), C. 1880

If one were even to set aside the intractable matter of identifying the nature of the affection that two anonymous men exhibited in a tender pose over a century ago, there are other, more rudimentary aspects of these photographs that elude definition. They often contain clues suggesting the kind of situations in which, according to social historians, intimate bonds between men would have flourished, such as in the army, navy, and merchant marines; in schools, colleges, and private clubs; on the frontier—in short, wherever men lived or worked apart from women. But problems invariably arise: How is one to know with any certainty that any given pair of men actually did pose within the circumstances suggested by the style of their clothing or by the scene depicted on the photographer's painted backdrop in front of which they so often sat? So many old photographs were created within the abstracting confines of photographic studios that provide little reliable information about locale. Consider, for example, a daguerreotype of a colorful pair who posed nonchalantly puffing on stogies during the

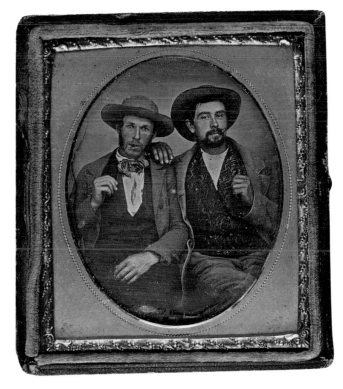

PHOTOGRAPHER UNKNOWN, SUBJECTS UNKNOWN, ⅙-PLATE DAGUERREOTYPE (3³/₄ × 3¹/₄″), C. 1850–55

83

early 1850s. Taken together, their broad-brimmed hats, unkempt facial hair, the macho swagger of their pose, and the way the fellow on the right wears vest and jacket over nothing more than an undershirt suggest "frontier" or "western locale." Ultimately, however, there is no way of knowing that these men actually did pose as one might imagine: in some dusty frontier outpost. This daguerreotype is therefore emblematic of a fundamental paradox inherent in old photographs whose origins are unknown: notwithstanding their wealth of visual data, their meaning cannot be fixed without the benefit of additional contextualizing information. "Individual images remain empty signs," Trachtenberg has noted, "unable to communicate a determinate meaning."[39]

Scholars have managed to identify the context, if not always the meaning, of many of the photographs of the men who headed west after news spread that on January 24, 1848, gold had been discovered at Sutter's Mill in California. Most of these photographs are daguerreotypes that show individuals posing forthrightly amid the attributes of the miner's trade: pickax and shovel, perhaps a pan for sifting through the sediment of streams and riverbeds, a knife, pistol, or rifle. Such portraits were often intended for loved ones back home for whom they functioned as treasured keepsakes. "Forty-niners" also posed in groups—for example, the eleven men who crowded into the frame of a half-plate daguerreotype by an unknown maker belonging to the Oakland Museum in California. It was not unusual in such group shots for men to pose with an arm around a friend's shoulder, as does the figure second from right in the top row of the Oakland photograph, whose hand rests on the shoulder of the man beside him. Altogether less conventional, and more striking, is the intimacy signaled by two hatless, fair-haired young men in the front row. The more relaxed of the two, second from left, has extended an arm around his more apprehensive comrade in an affectionate, even protective, gesture. More remarkable is the uniquely tender way in which the same man rests his other hand on top of his friend's, which rests comfortably on the former's knee. Although to this observer this seems a remarkably expressive—not to say suggestive—pose, judging from the essays in *Silver and Gold*—a catalogue that accompanied an ambitious exhibition of daguerreotypes documenting the gold rush—their authors evidently felt that it warranted no comment.

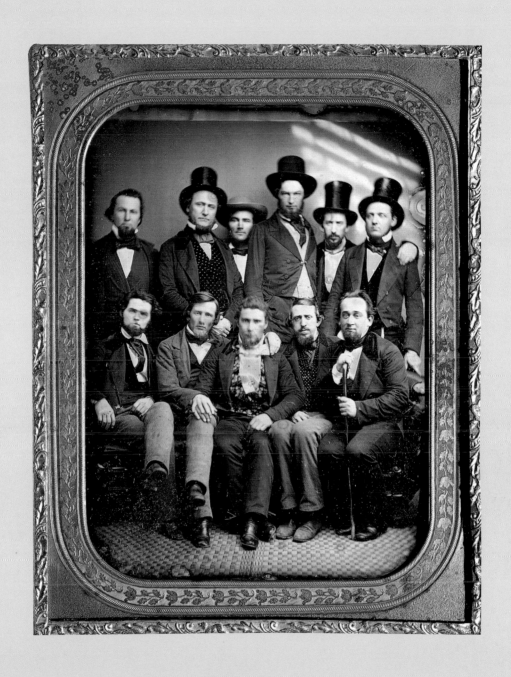

PHOTOGRAPHER UNKNOWN, *ELEVEN MEN WITH BEARDS, TOP HATS, AND VESTS,*
1/2-PLATE DAGUERREOTYPE (6 × 4³/4"), C. 1853

This daguerreotype is reproduced twice in the catalogue: first, as a frontispiece, where it appears as a close-up detail of the tender pair; second, in its entirety as one of the book's many plates. There, it is accompanied by a suggestive statement by a lawyer of the period, John McKrackan. "You cannot know the perfect freedom and independence that characterizes all our relationships," McKrackan writes. "Society if it exists [here] at all is freed from the multitude of prejudices and embarrassments and exactions that control the Eastern cities."[40] To be sure, the authors of the essays in *Silver and Gold* have a great deal to say about the hardships the miners endured, about their loneliness, and about the joy with which they greeted letters from mother, wife, or sweetheart back home. And while they tirelessly elucidate innumerable details of the exhibition's many daguerreotypes, they remain uncharacteristically silent regarding the intimacy displayed by some of the men in several of the photographs they are investigating. As for McKrackan's statement, it stands alone—its source undocumented, its implications uninvestigated. Does it allude to forms of affection between miners that might well have been the object of "prejudices and embarrassments and exactions that control the Eastern cities"? Or does it refer to other forms of prejudice, embarrassment, and exaction?

This silence regarding the affectionate poses adopted by some of the miners whose images survive to this day represents business-as-usual in the world of scholarly photo history, "serious" collection, and museum display. It is consistent with the way prominent collectors, connoisseurs, and historians have allowed this aspect of nineteenth-century American photography to go, if not unnoticed, then unremarked on. Evidently it occurred to no one involved in *Silver and Gold* to comment upon the visual evidence of same-sex affection, whether in relation to thirty years of published historical research into the tradition of romantic friendship between nineteenth-century American men and women or to more recently published documentary evidence of same-sex intimacy between miners during the California gold rush. The authors could, for example, have consulted a recently published study of the patterns of leisure and labor throughout the gold rush, wherein is noted the loneliness of the Eastern miners who traveled across the continent, and how that loneliness played itself out not only in the miners' pursuit of the region's relatively few Mexican, French, and Native-American women, but in romantic attachments and sexual attractions that arose between miners themselves.

For example, one miner, John Marshall Newton, was infatuated with a tall Dane, Hans. There were pronounced differences in the age, strength, and "inclination" of the two men, which helped foster a "cross-gendering" of the relationship they shared.[41]

The gold rush, with its promise of instant, though not easy, wealth, was only one of the enticements that lured American men away from stable family-centered lives. Both the gold rush and the frontier responded to the need that some men felt not only to escape the alienating effects of the industrialized workplace and the competitive marketplace, in which conviviality between men was rapidly disappearing, but to flee from other spaces in which women's authority interfered with their sense of masculine sovereignty.[42] For the establishment of women's authority was not entirely limited to the home. During the antebellum period, women extended their influence beyond domestic space to encompass educational and religious institutions as well. In this context, American manhood came to be defined, in part, as "the repudiation of the feminine, a resistance to mothers' and wives' efforts to civilize men." This oppositional process of self-definition also took on stylistic dimensions, as is evident in the prevalence of beards and mustaches among men who posed for photographs throughout this period.[43]

★   ★   ★

Romantic friendship between American men acquired a different kind of social prestige and meaning within the context of the Civil War. No sooner did young recruits leave the shelter and ties of home and family than they were thrust into the mutual dependence, care, and collective terror of being comrades in arms. Intimate ties were tacitly encouraged as a result of the soldier's need to steel himself for battle, to prepare emotionally for the prospect of injury and death, and for having to inflict such suffering on others. The need for group cohesion was especially pronounced within smaller "primary" groups, such as messmates, men from towns and townships who enlisted together, or single squads commanded by a sergeant. One historian notes that, bonded by common danger, "this primary group becomes a true band of brothers whose mutual dependence and mutual support create the cohesion necessary to function as a fighting unit." The soldiers' letters were less dry than this statement might suggest. "You would not believe that men could be so attached to each other," writes a soldier from the 1st Ohio Heavy Artillery. "We love each other like a band of brothers," notes another from the 11th Georgia. "We have suffered hardships and dangers together and are bound together by more than ordinary ties," writes a member of the 8th Texas Cavalry. "There is a feeling of love," writes a corporal in the 9th Alabama in October 1862, who had just returned to his regiment after convalescing at home from a wound inflicted during the Battle of Glendale. There is, he continues, "a strong attachment for those with whom one has shared common dangers, that is never felt for anyone else, or under any other circumstances."[44]

Just as Civil War soldiers were inclined to characterize their mutual affection in fraternal terms, the relations that bound enlisted men and commanding officers evoked the caring ties of fathers and sons. A captain in the 1st North Carolina described the greeting he received from his regiment after convalescence as "children [who] never wanted to see their father as much as they have wanted to see me." Similarly, enlisted men experienced the death of a beloved commanding officer as deep personal loss. "I lost my best friend in the army," wrote a private in the 124th New York. "Every man that knowde [sic] him loved him. . . . he never spoke a cross word to any of us. . . . I allways [sic] went to him when I wanted any thing money or aney thing [sic] else he never refused me." Given the intensity of the ties that developed between such soldiers, it is not surprising that even the promotion of a well-liked officer could induce happiness among his men for his good fortune, but, at the same time, they were "very sorry we had to part with him for he treated us so kindly I would rather be under him than any man in my knowing."[45]

Whitman, who for years had been advocating the "institution of the dear love of comrades," could experience the war as an official endorsement and sanctification of an agenda that may not have been "gay" but was clearly homoerotic. Whitman's wartime vocation was established when, in December 1862, he visited his brother George, a lieutenant in the 51st New York, who had been wounded at Fredericksburg. For three years, as a volunteer nurse, Walt Whitman comforted the injured, the sick, and the dying in military hospitals in and around Washington, D.C., and learned firsthand of the soldiers' suffering and bravery. The "wound

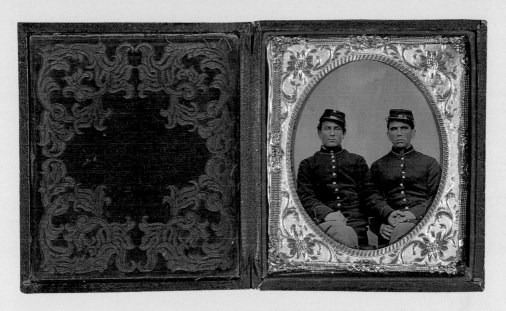

PHOTOGRAPHER UNKNOWN, SUBJECTS UNKNOWN, TINTYPE (3¾ × 3¼"), C. 1865

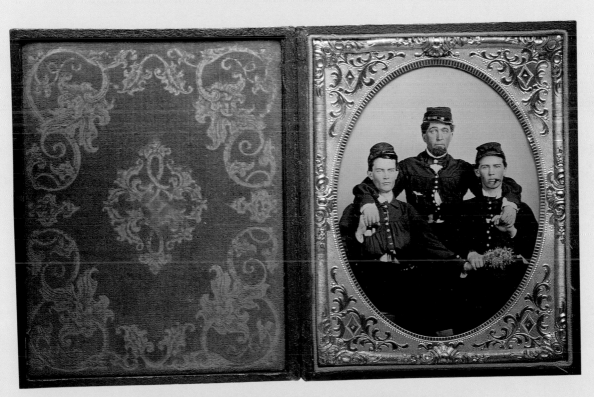

PHOTOGRAPHER UNKNOWN, SUBJECTS UNKNOWN, ½-PLATE AMBROTYPE (6 × 4¾"), C. 1863

dresser" was a role that appealed to the poet not only as patriotic but also as emotionally satisfying.

Whitman chronicled his memories of the variously tender and distressing times he spent in the company of courageous young men in letters and diary entries that he would later publish in *Specimen Days*. In one letter he wrote about his contact with a Mississippi officer in roguish, urbane terms, conjuring the notorious nightspots that enlivened the Bowery in Manhattan. "Our affection is quite an affair," he wrote, "quite romantic—sometimes when I lean over to say I am going, he puts his arm, &c., quite a scene for the New Bowery." In another, he described his ardent feelings for a soldier named Lewis K. Brown. "Lew is so good, so affectionate—when I came away, he reached up his face, I put my arm around him, and we gave each other a long kiss, half a minute long." Whitman proposed to yet another soldier that they live together after the war. "If anything should go wrong so that we do not meet again, here on earth," he wrote to Thomas P. Sawyer, "it seems to me (the way I feel now,) that my soul could never be happy, even in the world to come, without you, dear comrade."[46] He described the courage, dignity, and affection of a nineteen-year-old rebel amputee, "W.S.P. (2nd Maryland, Southern)," in a diary entry.

> *Evidently very intelligent and well-bred—very affectionate—held on to my hand, and put it by his face, not willing to let me leave. As I was lingering, soothing him in his pain, he says to me suddenly, "I hardly think you know who I am—I don't wish to impose upon you—I am a rebel soldier." I said I did not know that, but it made no difference. Visiting him daily for about two weeks after that, while he lived (death had marked him, and he was quite alone), I loved him much, always kissed him, and he did me.*[47]

More than a few of the men in Whitman's care chose to respond to the poet's kindness and generosity by giving him a portrait photograph of themselves—one of those cartes-de-visite whose manufacture Oliver Wendell Holmes had described in "Doings of the Sunbeam." Sometimes the grateful young men would add a simple inscription, for example: "Truly yours, Geo. B. Field," to which the poet would add as a further aide-mémoire a note describing the circumstances of the gift: "given me in Armory Sq. Hosp., March 12, 1865 by G.B.F., Ward A."[48] Although

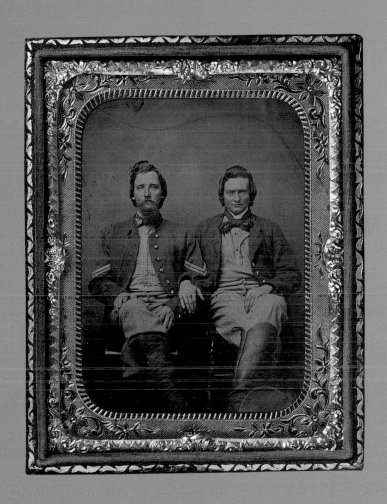

PHOTOGRAPHER UNKNOWN, SUBJECTS UNKNOWN, ¼-PLATE AMBROTYPE (4½ × 3½"), C. 1863

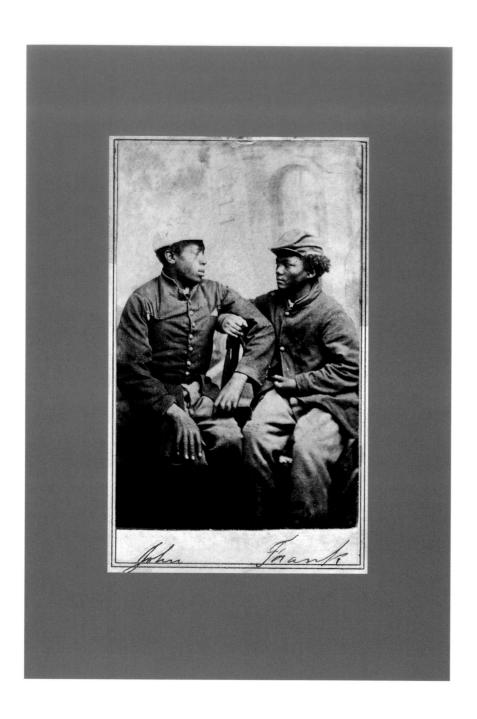

MCPHERSON & OLIVER (WILLIAM D. MCPHERSON), SUBJECTS UNKNOWN, CARTE DE VISITE (OVERALL: 4 × 2¹/₂″),
C. 1863. INSCRIBED: "JOHN" AND "FRANK." BACKMARK ON VERSO READS: "MCPHERSON & OLIVER PHOTOGRAPHERS"

more than a decade had passed since Horace Greeley identified photographic portraiture as the "current pledge of friendship," the introduction
of the card photograph actually dates from just before the beginning of
the Civil War. Indeed, the war proved a boon to the burgeoning photographic industry. On September 1, 1862, *Humphrey's Journal* noted that
"stock dealers are having it all their own way—recent calls for 600,000
more troops have given a prodigious impetus to the photographic business;
operators are getting desperate (no supplies) and dealers have advanced
prices."[49] Itinerant photographers followed armies from one encampment
to another, setting up their horse-drawn photo studios and darkrooms,
making it possible for soldiers to buy inexpensive likenesses. Tintypes
proved an especially popular photographic medium at such encamp-
ments, in part because of their durability, in part because the medium did
not require the production of prints. During the summer of 1862, a war
correspondent from the New York *Tribune* reported from Fredericksburg:

> *A camp is hardly pitched before one of the omnipresent artists in collodi-*
> *on and amber-bead varnish drives up his two horse wagon, pitches his*
> *canvas-gallery and unpacks his chemicals. Our army here is now so large*
> *that quite a company of these gentlemen have gathered about us. The*
> *amount of business they find is remarkable. Their tents are thronged from*
> *morning to night, and while the day lasteth, their golden harvest runs*
> *on. Here, for instance, near General Burnside's headquarters, there are*
> *the combined establishments of two brothers from Pennsylvania, who*
> *rejoice in the wonderful name "Bergstresser". They have followed the*
> *army for more than a year, and since they came here, they took in one of*
> *the galleries, so I am told, 160 odd pictures at $1.00 (on which the net*
> *profit was probably ninety-five cents each).*[50]

To judge from the surviving visual evidence, not all soldiers chose to
pose alone. On the contrary, many commemorated the close ties they
forged as dear comrades by posing together. Just how cheaply such photographs could be procured is evident not only in the great numbers of
them that survive to this day, but in the range of men who posed in
them. These include two freed slaves who fought in one of the African-
American regiments, and whose given names, "John" and "Frank," are
inscribed directly under their portrait, which in all likelihood was shot in
Baton Rouge, Louisiana, in 1863.[51]

Not all American men had to relocate to the frontier in order to find ways of reconstituting an embattled masculinity or of replacing the soulless rivalry of the marketplace with the homosocial warmth of comradely love. Throughout the nineteenth century, fraternal organizations such as the American Freemasons, the Independent Order of Odd Fellows, the Knights of Pythias, and the Improved Order of Red Men created private spaces and secret rituals in which certain aspects of home and church could be adapted away from the emasculating presence of mothers and wives. Writing about "Secret Societies in America" in 1897, W. S. Harwood estimated that of a total adult male population of nineteen million, as many as five and a half million American men belonged to such fraternal organizations. Harwood referred to the last third of the nineteenth century as the "Golden Age of Fraternity." More recently, the extraordinary appeal of fraternal orders has been attributed to the Byzantine elaborations of the secret initiation rituals, whose "sudden diffusion and proliferation" is placed somewhat earlier, to the period 1820–50.[52]

The extent to which the lodges borrowed from the language of family relationships offers one clue to the symbolic significance of the fraternal orders and their carefully scripted rituals. Not only did members refer to each other as "brothers," but officers were called "fathers," and initiates "sons." Inasmuch as the initiation ritual constituted a symbolic form of rebirth into the fraternal family, the initiate's sense of self—itself a product of socialization by women—had to be undermined before he could be born again. Initiates were therefore not infrequently subjected to forms of ritual humiliation. They were blindfolded, sometimes dressed in specially designed costumes, sometimes stripped down to a loincloth or apron. In a ritual dating from 1868, the New Order of Redmen took to calling their initiates "squaws." The initiate was forced to lie face down on the floor before a member-guide led him blindly on a symbolic journey through shadowy torch-lit chambers, while other members chanted or sang hymns in the background. Such rites of passage were intended to test the resolve of the proposed new member. The perilous nature of the challenge he confronted was heightened through a blend of melodramatic rhetoric and stagecraft. Initiation rituals eventually reached a dramatic

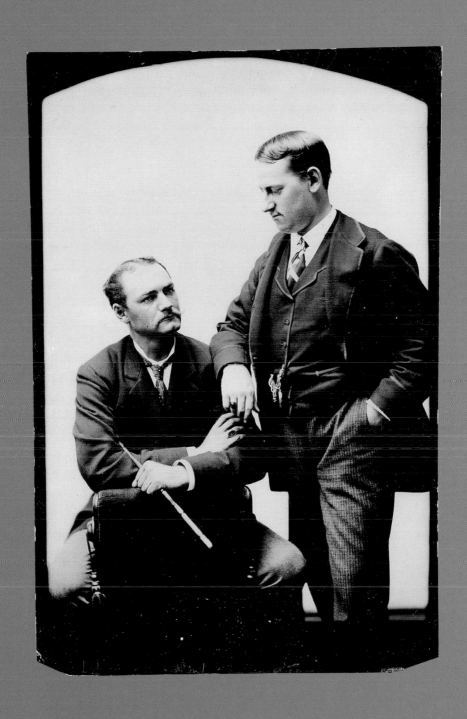

PHOTOGRAPHER UNKNOWN, SUBJECTS UNKNOWN, CABINET CARD (6¹/₂ × 4¹/₄"), C. 1890

climax in which initiates were forced to contemplate their mortality in a confrontation with a coffin containing a skeleton, or to play a role not unlike the biblical Isaac's in a ritual sacrifice by the father of his son. But just as the Hebrew God intervened to prevent Abraham from taking Isaac's life, one of the "fathers" of the lodge would intercede to recognize the initiate's mettle and welcome him into the fold.

Such rites, and the all-male spaces in which they were staged, offered young American men a method for distancing themselves from the inhibiting influence of mothers and wives, and thereby of facilitating their entry into the world of men. This is not to say, however, that fraternal orders altogether eradicated values, tastes, and tasks that had been identified with the female social sphere. On the contrary. Not unlike the "wild man" rites of the contemporary men's movement with its drum beating, sweat lodges, and heartfelt confessions of father love, the fraternal movement made it possible for late-nineteenth-century American men to entertain values, tastes, and tasks that they would otherwise have had to disavow as feminine. Thus, one may point to the frequency with which members of fraternal orders published sentimental tributes to mothers and mother love, the fussy extravagance of fraternal fashions with their aprons and elaborately embroidered robes, the lodges' participation in charitable activities, and their discouragement of drinking among members. Inasmuch as the peak of fraternal expansion arguably dates from the last quarter of the nineteenth century, one might also suggest that their social prominence reflected the "widening chasm between men" and its consequent production of "a deep yearning for the intimacies that had earlier marked men's lives."[53] As the century drew to a close and intimate ties between men came under increasing scrutiny, the lodges offered an institutional guarantee of deniability. Not unlike the military and athletic teams of the twentieth century, they sought to ensure that the same-sex affection they encouraged would not be taken for the wrong kind.

★　　★　　★

Throughout much of the nineteenth century the construction and maintenance of romantic friendship as "pure" found support in the tacit understanding of love and lust as different things. Before Freud

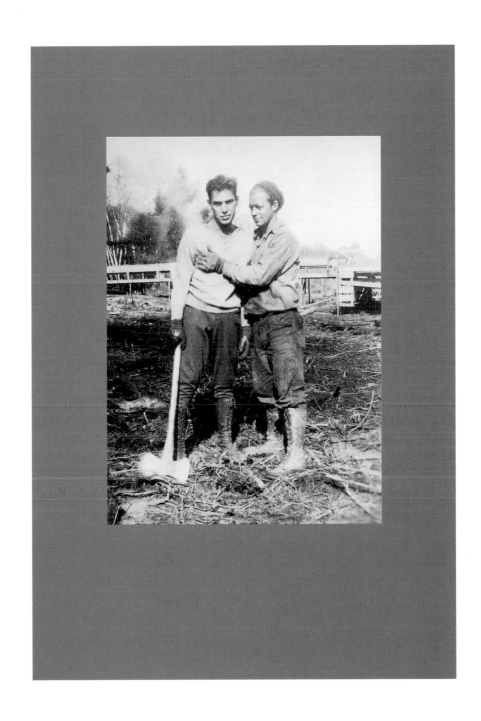

PHOTOGRAPHER UNKNOWN, SUBJECTS UNKNOWN, GELATIN SILVER PRINT (2³/₄ × 2″), C. 1910

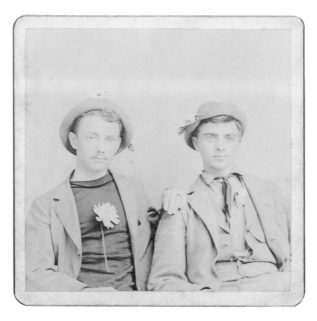

A. J. BLOOM, SUBJECTS UNKNOWN, ALBUMEN PRINT MOUNTED ON BOARD (3 × 3″), C. 1900. INSCRIPTION ON VERSO READS: "ERNEST AND LEN." BACKMARK ON VERSO READS: "A. J. BLOOM, ANDOVER, N.J."

proposed the sex drive as the universal motive force in human life, love could be regarded as other than eros. This meant that romantic friends could enjoy considerable latitude in the emotional and physical expression of their affections. According to one gay historian, "The secure belief in the idea of a nonsexual 'passion' made possible the unself-conscious, unembarrassed expression of same-sex attraction, clearly including a sensual component."[54]

The understanding of homosexuality and heterosexuality as barely century-old social constructions should not, however, obscure the fact that the activities most intimately associated with homosexuality were widely condemned and harshly punished since well before the dawn of modernity.[55] In addition to the distinction between passionate love and lust, the survival of romantic friendship also depended on the exclusion of "sodomy" from public life and bourgeois discourse. Although "sodomy" denoted different forms of forbidden behavior at different moments throughout the nineteenth century in the United States, during most of the century this religiously freighted term referred to anal sex between men, but also to "various nonprocreative sexual acts, including oral sex and masturbation."[56] Indeed, masturbation was something of an obsession among mid-nineteenth-century moral reformers such as Orson Fowler, R. T. Trall, and Samuel Bayard Woodward, whose advice pamphlets targeting young people and their parents were best-sellers from their dates of publication during the mid-1850s through their many later nineteenth-century reprints. To read these publications is to realize that nineteenth-century Americans could identify, and did disparage, certain traits that only later would be cobbled together to form the stereotypical figure of the modern homosexual.

One of the more popular tracts, Fowler's *Amativeness* (1856), was named for the predisposition of some people to "sensuality" and "self pollution" that phrenologists such as Fowler and his brother Lorenzo identified by detecting bumps on specific parts of a person's head. The Fowlers were the principal American promoters of phrenology, the pseudo-science that thrived in the United States during the mid-nineteenth century. Along with their business partner, Samuel Wells, the Fowlers published scores of books on the subject. They also operated a significant tourist attraction on Nassau Street in lower Manhattan known as the "Phrenological Cabinet." There, visitors surveyed the latest phrenological publications and examined the skulls of "murderers, thieves . . . lions, tigers, hyenas, dangerous lunatics, savage tribesmen" for all the outward signs of the traits that supposedly defined their character. One visitor to the Phrenological Cabinet during the 1840s was the young journalist and editor Walt Whitman, who worked nearby. For three dollars Lorenzo Fowler agreed to survey Whitman's own head in 1849. On a phrenological scale of from one to seven, Fowler measured the size of such organs as Amativeness (6), Philoprogentiveness (6–7), Self-Esteem (6), Destructiveness (5–6), Cautiousness (6), and Adhesiveness (6)—this last being his predisposition to friendship.[57] Six years later, Fowler and Wells published the first edition of *Leaves of Grass*.

In *Amativeness*, Fowler advised readers to keep the "sensual," or amative, instinct under control so that body and mind might achieve the proper equilibrium necessary to fulfill their "legitimate design."[58] Whitman was influenced by Fowler's model of mental and physical equilibrium, so much so that in 1870 he wrote a famously tortured journal entry in which he resolves to curtail his attraction to—or at any rate his pursuit of—Peter Doyle, whom one historian describes as the "love of his life."[59]

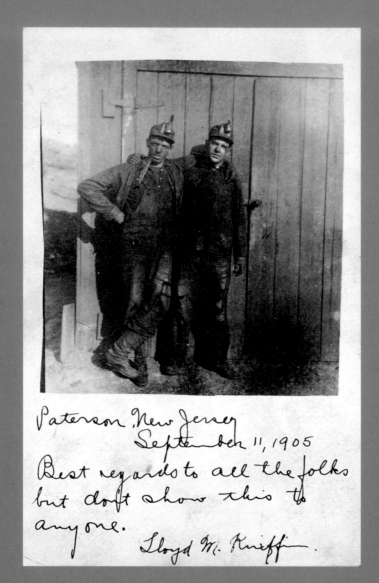

PHOTOGRAPHER UNKNOWN, SUBJECTS UNKNOWN, GELATIN SILVER PRINT, REAL PHOTO POSTCARD (5¹/₂ × 3¹/₂"), 1905.
INSCRIPTION READS: "PATERSON, NEW JERSEY/SEPTEMBER 11, 1905/BEST REGARDS TO ALL THE FOLKS/BUT DON'T
SHOW THIS TO/ANYONE./LLOYD M. KNIEFF [?]." INSCRIPTION ON VERSO READS: SAMUEL HUNTER
ESQ./DUCKTOWN/POLK CO./TENNESSEE." POSTMARKED: SEPTEMBER 12, 1905

Like so much about romantic friendship in the nineteenth century, Whitman's journal entry, which today reads like the tormented ravings of a closeted gay man, must be understood within the terms of its own historical context. Those terms were dictated to Whitman by phrenology—right down to the extravagant use of the upper case.

TO GIVE UP ABSOLUTELY for good, from the present hour, this FEVERISH, FLUCTUATING, useless, UNDIGNIFIED PURSUIT of 16.4 [Peter Doyle]—too long, (much too long) persevered in,— so humiliating— —It must come at last & had better come now—(It cannot possibly be a success) LET THERE FROM THIS HOUR BE NO FALTERING, NO GETTING at all henceforth, (NOT ONCE, under any circumstances)—avoid seeing her [originally "him"], or meeting her, or any talk or explanations—or ANY MEETING WHATEVER FROM THIS HOUR FORTH, FOR LIFE July 15 '70

. . . . Depress the adhesive nature
It is in excess—making life a torment
Ah this diseased, feverish, disproportionate adhesiveness.[60]

The popularity of phrenology—the appeal of its promise to find the innermost traits of human beings cast on the surface of the head—suggests the anxieties and fears that beset Americans throughout this period of rapid social transformation. As Smith-Rosenberg has maintained, some Americans clearly celebrated "the individualism and freedom from structure [that] they found in Jacksonian America," but many others feared the unraveling of the "hierarchical world order," which was evident in the altered social relations within families and the workplace, in a sense of "formlessness and insecurity," a sense of loss of control.[61] Just as fathers were helpless to arrest the economic developments that continued to undermine family cohesion and parental authority, so they were unable to control the behavior of sons once they left home, whether to find work in professions that differed from their own or to attend boarding and day schools. One result of these changes was that the adolescent male became a point of convergence for fears and anxieties that beset Americans at mid-century. This anxious convergence was evident in the proliferation and popularity of self-help tracts like Fowler's.

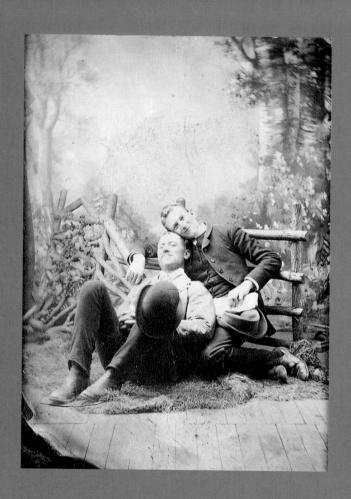

PHOTOGRAPHER UNKNOWN, SUBJECTS UNKNOWN, TINTYPE (3³⁄₈ × 2¹⁄₂″), C. 1880

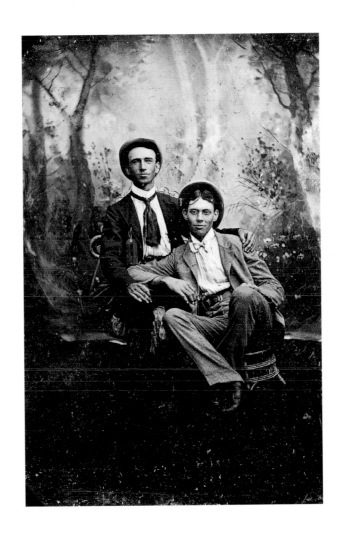

PHOTOGRAPHER UNKNOWN, SUBJECTS UNKNOWN, TINTYPE (3³/₄ × 2³/₈″), C. 1880

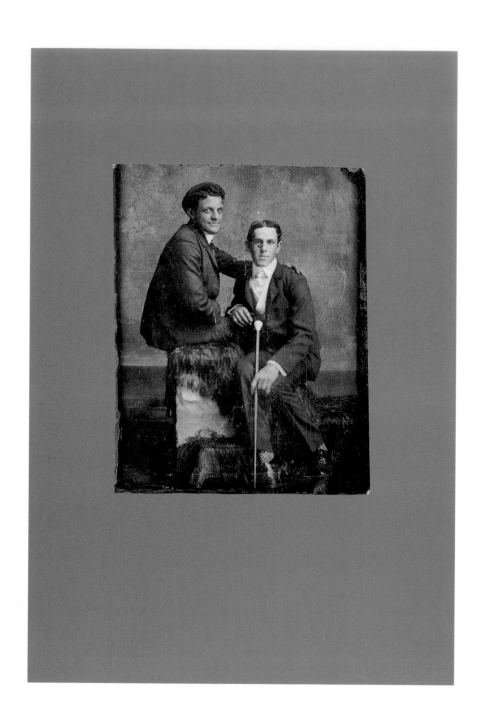

PHOTOGRAPHER UNKNOWN, SUBJECTS UNKNOWN, TINTYPE (3$\frac{1}{4}$ × 2$\frac{5}{8}$″), C. 1885

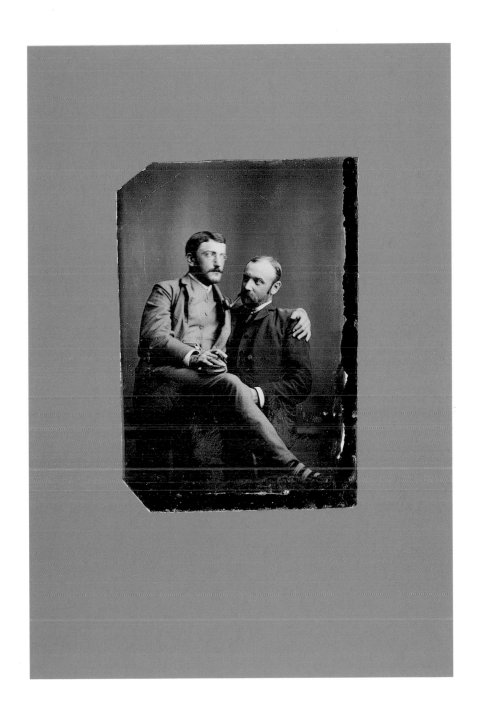

PHOTOGRAPHER UNKNOWN, SUBJECTS UNKNOWN, TINTYPE (3¹/₂ × 2¹/₂″), C. 1890

Therefore, in *Amativeness* Fowler devotes a great deal of attention to the situation of the many youths who were spending much of their time at boarding and day schools. Like other mid-century moral reformers, Fowler regarded these recent additions to the American social scene as sources of "untold mischief." He therefore offered helpful hints to parents and teachers as to how to police the young; for example, how to detect whether or not youths were prone to "sensuality" in general, and to masturbation in particular. Fowler instructs the reader to take note of boys who are "carrying the hands frequently to the organs by way of changing their position." He cautions boys about the grave perils of "self-abuse." To read certain items on this seemingly endless list of hazards is to realize the extent to which Victorians did not need to await the later nineteenth-century naming of the "invert" or "homosexual" to identify and condemn as abnormal those traits that would be grouped together to form the stereotypical homosexual. After advising that masturbation injures health, exhausts the body, enfeebles the mind, and "inflames the whole system," Fowler adds that it "deteriorates the sexual characteristics," which is to say that it "impairs the manliness of the male, and the feminineness of the female." In his contemporaneous *Home-Treatment for Sexual Abuses: A Practical Treatise* (1856), R. T. Trall provides a more vivid representation of the behavior and even the appearance of the masturbator, one that leaves no doubt that he is none other than the as-yet-unnamed homosexual. The masturbator is "timid, afraid of his own shadow, uncertain . . . nor will he walk erect or dignified as if conscious of his manhood and lofty in his aspirations, but will walk more with a diminutive cringing, sycophantic, inferior, mean, self-debased manner."[62] The absence of the modern category of the homosexual did not prevent nineteenth-century Americans from identifying and condemning the effeminate male. By the same token, the mid-nineteenth-

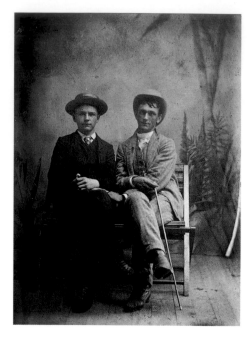

PHOTOGRAPHER UNKNOWN, SUBJECTS UNKNOWN, TINTYPE (3¼ × 2⅝"), C. 1880

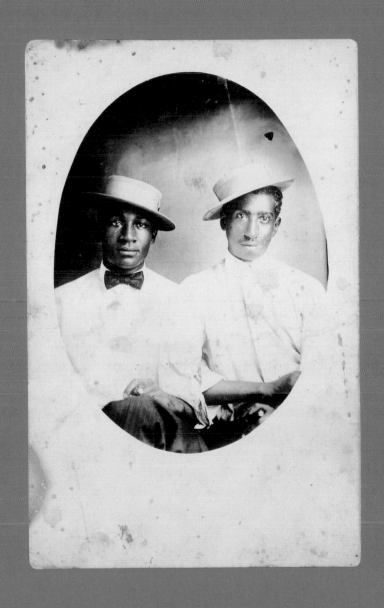

PHOTOGRAPHER UNKNOWN, SUBJECTS UNKNOWN, GELATIN SILVER PRINT,
REAL PHOTO POSTCARD (5$^{1}/_{2}$ × 3$^{1}/_{2}$″), C. 1905

century grasp of effeminacy in men and of masculinity in women as abnormal and worthy of condemnation can be seen to summon from medical science the categorization of sexual difference, if for no other reason than to rationalize and justify its continued social stigmatization and marginalization.

★   ★   ★

The popularity of the photographic pledge of friendship, and of the sentiment it conveyed, would show no signs of diminishing as long as romantic friendship continued to thrive. The more fervent manifestations of romantic friendship may actually have benefited from the fact that bourgeois power and influence achieved hegemonic political, economic, and social influence in the United States and throughout much of Europe during the middle of the nineteenth century. Not only did the attendant rise of wage labor and the continued segregation of the sexes, classes, and races help to foster such bonds, but it was also consistent with bourgeois style—"a mixture," in Peter Gay's formulation, "of delicate euphemisms and wide-eyed candor"—that sodomy would remain so far beyond the pale, not only of acceptable middle-class behavior but of polite discussion as well. Indeed, as a topic, it could barely enter language. Thus, "the abominable and revolting crime," or "the crime that cannot be named." Paradoxically, the most repressive aspects of bourgeois discretion yielded liberal dividends for romantic friends and their fellow travelers. "Behind the sheltering facade of discretion many nineteenth-century male and female homosexuals, defining their own forbidden ways of loving, enjoyed a privileged space of impunity for their unorthodox amorous arrangements."[63]

But as homosexuality became an increasingly prominent topic of public discussion and an object of legislative initiative and medical and psychological examination, the bourgeois inclination to disavow such behavior—attributing it instead to dissolute aristocrats, foreigners, and atavistic members of the working class—became untenable. And if scandal in the ranks of the middle class could no longer be denied, then the sinner would have to be punished. Thus the modern demonization of same-sex love found its culminating public instance during the spring of 1895 in the sensationally reported trials and subsequent imprisonment of

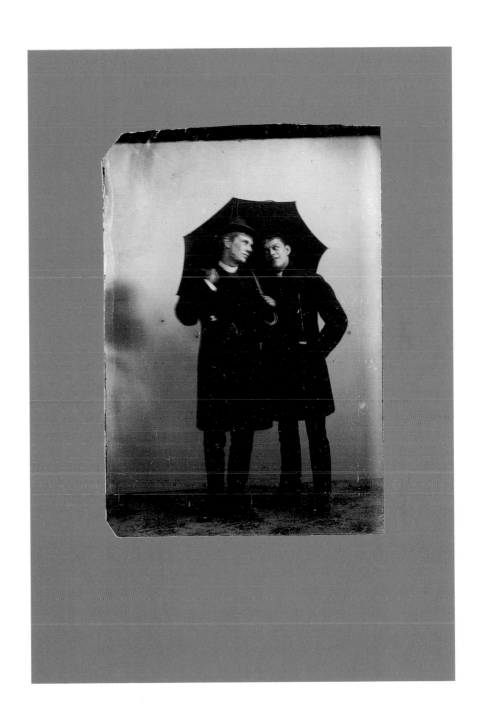

PHOTOGRAPHER UNKNOWN, SUBJECTS UNKNOWN, TINTYPE (3$\frac{1}{4}$ × 2$\frac{1}{4}$"), C. 1890

Oscar Wilde—a man whose wit and superior attitude had already supplied the most powerful classes in Great Britain with ample reason to take offense. Thirteen years earlier, in March and May 1882, the twenty-eight-year-old Wilde—then on his famous North American tour—made two pilgrimages to Camden, New Jersey, to visit Walt Whitman, whose poems he claimed to have been reading since the age of twelve. Before Wilde left, the poet gave him a pair of photographs of himself—one for him, the other to be given to Swinburne.[64]

The passage of such laws as Great Britain's 1885 Labouchère Amendment to the Criminal Law Amendment Act has assumed emblematic significance. Unlike previous legislation, which had outlawed "sodomy and buggery"—regardless of the sex of whoever was caught in the act—the Labouchère Amendment cast a finer net over a more narrowly delineated segment of the population as it criminalized "any male person" who commits "any act of gross indecency with another male person."[65] As it prohibited all acts that men might engage in together, including many that previously were practiced with impunity by "romantic friends," the new law contributed to the social construction of the homosexual as explicitly criminal. Within the context of other discursive developments that were also heightening the homosexual's public profile, the chilling effect of this legislation proved sufficiently pointed to take on cultural dimensions. For example, the increasingly pronounced (not to say desperate) inclination to turn to the classical past for an "apologia of a fateful inheritance" was not the only means by which Whitman's admirer, John Addington Symonds, sought to legitimize his sexual needs, which then more than ever he had reason to regard as shameful. It was in 1890 that Symonds turned for cultural validation to that erstwhile champion of urban cruising and manly love, Whitman, whose famous disavowal is not, as we shall see, the only proof of the bard's growing sense of guilt as the century, and his life, were drawing to a close.[66] Reflecting on the social consequences of the Wilde trials, W. D. Stead, the primary author of the Labouchère Amendment, acknowledged the destructive effects of the scandalous trial, if not of the legislation that arguably laid the groundwork for it. In a letter to the author, socialist, and popular sexologist Edward Carpenter, he noted: "A few more cases like Oscar Wilde's and we should find the freedom of comradeship now possible to men seriously impaired to the permanent detriment of the race."[67]

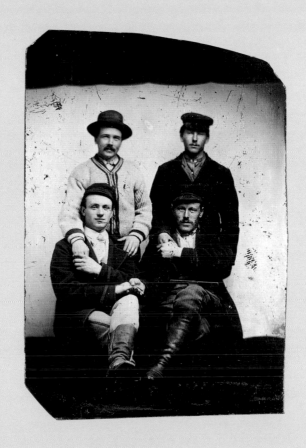

PHOTOGRAPHER UNKNOWN, SUBJECTS UNKNOWN, TINTYPE (4 × 2³/₄"), C. 1875

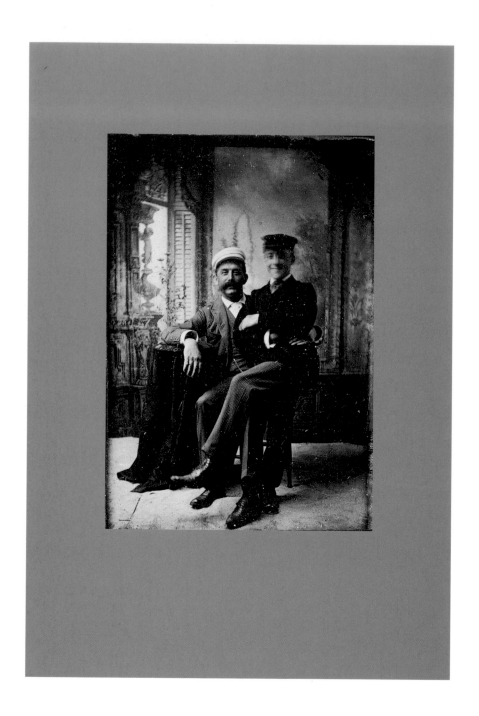

PHOTOGRAPHER UNKNOWN, SUBJECTS UNKNOWN, TINTYPE (3³/₈ × 2¹/₄″), C. 1880

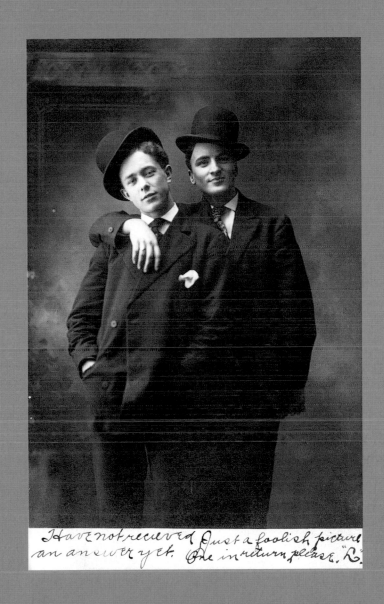

PHOTOGRAPHER UNKNOWN, SUBJECTS UNKNOWN, GELATIN SILVER PRINT, REAL PHOTO POSTCARD (5½ × 3½"), 1907.
INSCRIPTION READS: "HAVE NOT RECEIVED/AN ANSWER YET./JUST A FOOLISH PICTURE./ONE IN RETURN PLEASE. 'L.'"
POSTMARKED ON VERSO: "FORD [?] CITY, APRIL 13 PM 1907"

In the United States, no federal antisodomy statutes existed during the nineteenth nor, for that matter, during the twentieth century. Instead, such laws have always been left for individual states to decide. (Thus in *Bowers v. Hardwick* [1986], the Supreme Court affirmed the states' rights to maintain sodomy statutes.) But in accordance with religious injunctions, many states outlawed sodomy throughout the nineteenth century. Significantly, it was only at the end of the nineteenth century, after the naming and the stigmatization of the homosexual, that the State of New York outlawed "consenting to sodomy"—a broader application that targets the person as much as the act.

Even as modern legislation like the Labouchère Amendment constructed the homosexual as criminal, doctors and practitioners in the burgeoning social sciences, in sexology and psychology, were defining same-sexers as atavistic, deviant, and pathological, in opposition to the emerging heterosexual norm.[68] As a result of this convergence of overlapping institutional and disciplinary developments, a wide range of emotions and behaviors between men, which previously had been cherished within the context of romantic friendship, were increasingly identified with crime and sexual "perversion." As we have seen, throughout much of the nineteenth century, social relations forged by industrialized capitalism had combined with traditional gender assignments to segregate the sexes, races, and classes, and to foster same-sex romantic friendship. But toward the century's end, the modern institutional and disciplinary innovations helped advance a more restrictive heterosexuality as the social norm. As a result, it became necessary to ensure that the intense, libidinally charged relations between men that still electrified the homosocial hubs of exclusively male learning and labor not only would *not* be construed as "homosexual" but would as well spark an incendiary homophobia. And as the queer theorist Eve Sedgwick has demonstrated, the institution of homophobia within the context of homosocial male bonding proved instrumental to the consolidation and maintenance of male power and privilege at a time when increasing numbers of women—from Elizabeth Cady Stanton and Susan B. Anthony to Sojourner Truth—were contesting that birthright by demanding the rights of full citizenship.[69]

The institution of normative sexuality did not abruptly eliminate the tradition of romantic friendship in the United States. Toward the end of Whitman's life the poet considered many of the infamous "Calamus" poems conventional enough to include them in the 1886 and 1892 editions of *Leaves of Grass*—editions that one historian has described as "scrubbed, polite." Thus, the "comradely love" that Whitman had always been careful to define in conformity with socially acceptable standards still fit snugly within mainstream conventions—this despite the best efforts of Anthony Comstock, whose draconian obscenity laws were intended to suppress *Leaves of Grass*, among many other works.[70] Similarly, the new terminology of sexual difference only gradually seeped into the consciousness of most Americans. Recent historical research has revealed the existence of a distinct class of homosexually active, effeminate American men who were recognized as "fairies" from at least the 1870s when Billy McGlory, proprietor of a Bowery dance hall, hired these exotic individuals for his establishment. The fairy was also described at that time in a guide to the social geography of New York, and was tolerated by much of working-class society, which regarded him as "an anomaly, certainly, but as more amusing than abhorrent, and only rarely as a threat to the gender order." So obviously was he "a different species of human being," the historian George Chauncey maintains, "that his very effeminacy served to confirm rather than threaten the masculinity of other men."[71]

In the late nineteenth century, a compelling conjunction took place between the technical history of photography and the history of modern social control. As human beings were for the first time being classified in terms of their "good" and "bad" sexual object choice, the self-produced snapshot was invented. Insofar as the technology that enabled self-made photographs circumvented the public scrutiny implicit in a visit to the commercial photography studio, it facilitated the proliferation of informal poses and of private, potentially "antisocial" images such as pornography. The correspondence of these seemingly unrelated developments brings to mind the "panoptic" disciplinary regime that Michel Foucault identified with the emergence of modern, liberalizing methods of maintaining order in societies that had progressed from absolutist to democratic forms of government. Foucault derived the term "panoptic" from the name that the English social reformer Jeremy Bentham gave to his late-eighteenth-century design for the modern prison. In their historical correspondence, the technical invention of the self-produced photograph and the social construction of the homosexual demonstrate how modern social control is maintained. Rather than imposing order from above through the

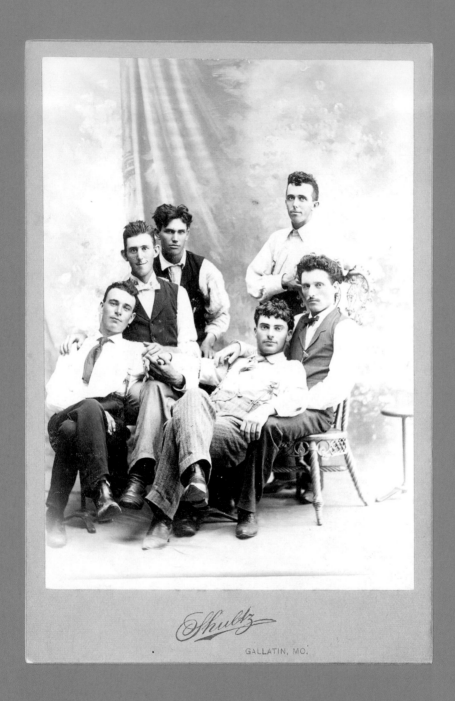

SHULTZ, SUBJECTS UNKNOWN, CABINET CARD (6½ × 4¼"), C. 1885–90. EMBOSSED:

"SHULTZ/GALLATIN, MO." INSCRIPTION ON VERSO READS: "PEARLY MACY'S 'FRIENDS'"

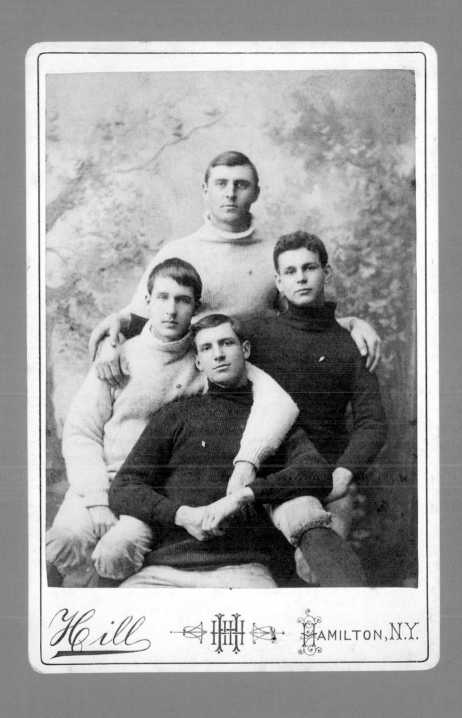

HILL, SUBJECTS UNKNOWN, CABINET CARD (6$\frac{1}{2}$ × 4$\frac{1}{4}$"), C. 1890. IMPRINT READS: "HILL/HAMILTON, NY"

unwieldy imposition of brute force, antisocial behavior is deterred through the infinitely more subtle and cost-effective process of instituting normative sexuality.[72]

Geopolitical events also contributed to the persistence, or revival, of passionate friendships between men. Just as the Civil War encouraged and sanctified comradely love, World War I generated intimate ties between soldiers who also commemorated their bonds by posing affectionately before the camera. There is ample photographic evidence of the affection that thrived between doughboys who confronted annihilation in unspeakable conditions far from home. But in post-Labouchère Britain, the sanction granted comradely love in wartime was countered by efforts at containment that reflected the institution of normative sexuality. In the second volume of Pat Barker's fact-based World War I trilogy, *The Eye in the Door*, one shell-shocked officer, the patrician Charles Manning, addresses this predicament during a session with his psychiatrist, Dr. William Rivers: "In war," Manning says, "there's this enormous glorification of love between men, and yet at the same time it arouses anxiety. Is it the right kind of love? Well, one way to make sure it's the right kind is to make public disapproval of the other kind crystal clear. And then there's pleasure in killing—." In an author's note, Barker recounts the historical efforts of British MP Noel Pemberton Billing, whose newspaper, the *Imperialist* (later the *Vigilante*), published an article in January 1918 entitled "The First 47,000," a homophobic diatribe ghostwritten in Billing's name by the British intelligence agent Captain Harold Spencer. The exposé claimed to uncover a massive conspiracy of influential British homosexuals with intimate ties to "a certain German Prince." A subsequent article, "The Cult of the Clitoris," also purporting to have been written by Billing, suggested that the list of subscribers to a private performance of Oscar Wilde's *Salome* included many names from the "47,000." That evening's Salome, the actress Maud Allen, sued Billing for libel, since the article clearly implied that she was a lesbian. The subsequent trial was presided over by Lord Justice Darling, who lost control of the proceedings after being identified himself as one of the 47,000, but not before Lord Alfred Douglas, Oscar Wilde's infamous Bosie, testified against Wilde's devoted friend and literary executor, Robert Ross, identifying him as "the leader of all the sodomites in London."[73]

In the United States the intense homosocial effects of World War I also occasioned homophobic public policies. In 1916, for the first time in

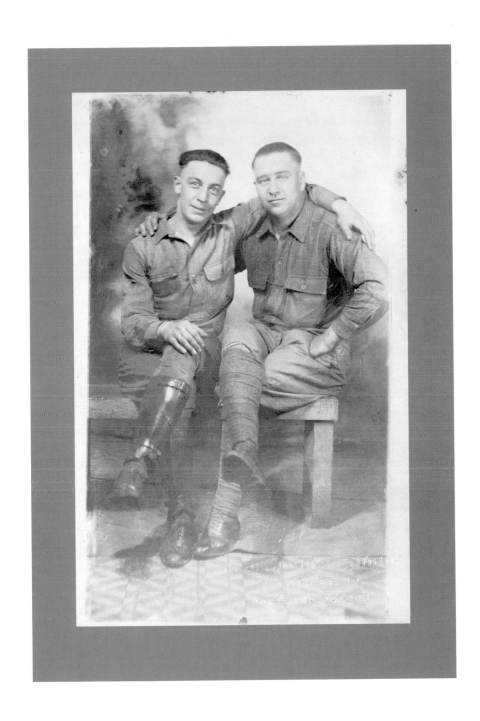

PROF. JOHN'S STUDIO, SUBJECTS UNKNOWN, GELATIN SILVER PRINT, REAL PHOTO POSTCARD (5½ × 3½"), C. 1915.
EMBOSSED: "PROF. JOHN'S STUDIO/71-5TH ST. NO./PORTLAND, OREGON"

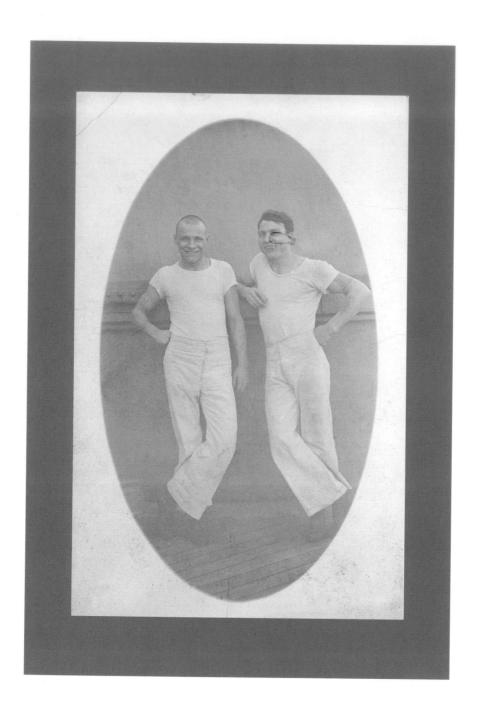

PHOTOGRAPHER UNKNOWN, SUBJECTS UNKNOWN, GELATIN SILVER PRINT, REAL PHOTO POSTCARD (5½ × 3½"), 1916.
INSCRIPTION ON VERSO READS: "FROM BUTCH KIMMEL [ILLEG.] TO FRANK/TAKEN AT CAALEBRA P.R./JAN. 20TH 1916"

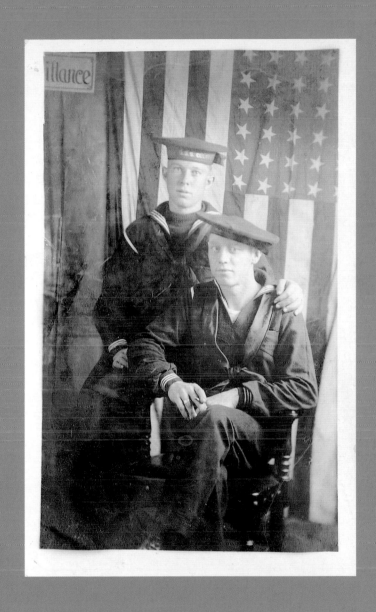

PHOTOGRAPHER UNKNOWN, SUBJECTS UNKNOWN, GELATIN SILVER PRINT, REAL PHOTO POSTCARD (5$^{1}/_{2}$ × 3$^{1}/_{2}$"), C. 1905

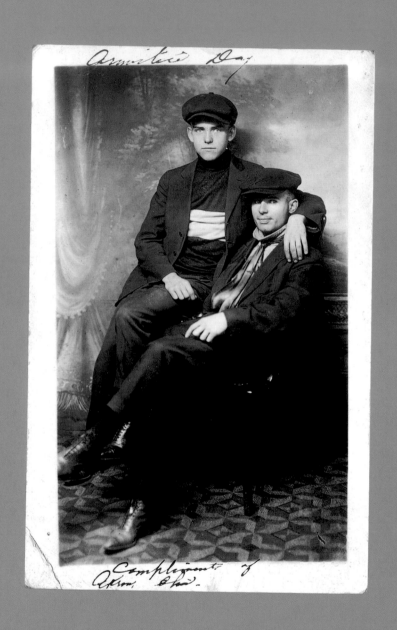

PHOTOGRAPHER UNKNOWN, SUBJECTS UNKNOWN, GELATIN SILVER PRINT, REAL PHOTO POSTCARD (5½ × 3½"), 1918.

INSCRIPTION AT TOP READS: "ARMISTICE DAY"; AT BOTTOM: "COMPLIMENTS OF AKRON OHIO"

a century, the Articles of War were amended to declare assault with the intent to commit sodomy as a felony crime. Three years later, they were amended yet again to name sodomy itself a felony. Since the crime was no longer assault but the sex act itself, sailors and soldiers were imprisoned for five or six years for engaging in consensual sex. The idea of screening to eliminate gay and lesbian recruits from the ranks of the American military also dates to World War I, when it was advanced by practitioners in the emerging field of psychiatry. Thus Dr. Albert Abrams wrote in September 1918 that while "recruiting the elements which make up our invincible army, we cannot ignore what is obvious and which will militate against the combative prowess of our forces in this war. . . . From a military viewpoint, the homosexualist is not only dangerous, but an ineffective fighter. . . . It is imperative that homosexualists be recognized by military authorities." Shortly after the armistice that ended World War I, the strategy of entrapment to purge the military of homosexuals was inaugurated in Rhode Island by Chief Machinist's Mate Ervin Arnold, a former police investigator. With the approval of his superiors, Arnold persuaded seven enlisted men to entrap other enlisted men whom they suspected of being gay.[74]

★   ★   ★

There are so many surviving photographs that commemorate affectionate ties between nineteenth- and early-twentieth-century American men that confronting them en masse can seem overwhelming. In an attempt to make sense of the photographic array, I make copies of originals that I've borrowed from collectors and pin them to a work surface in clusters that reflect the varied categories that come to my mind. Some of these categories pertain to recurring poses: photographs in which men stand with arms on each other's shoulders, or in which one stands while the other sits; in which they hold hands or entwine their legs while seated; in which one sits on the lap of the other, or one reclines against the supporting body of his mate, or one embraces the other from behind. Other categories pertain to context. There are photographs that appear to have been taken in recreational settings, especially by the sea, with sitters resplendent in bathing costumes or other picturesque, leisure-time apparel. In other photographs, vocation is of preeminent importance: thus farmers, factory workers, or tram- and railway conductors.

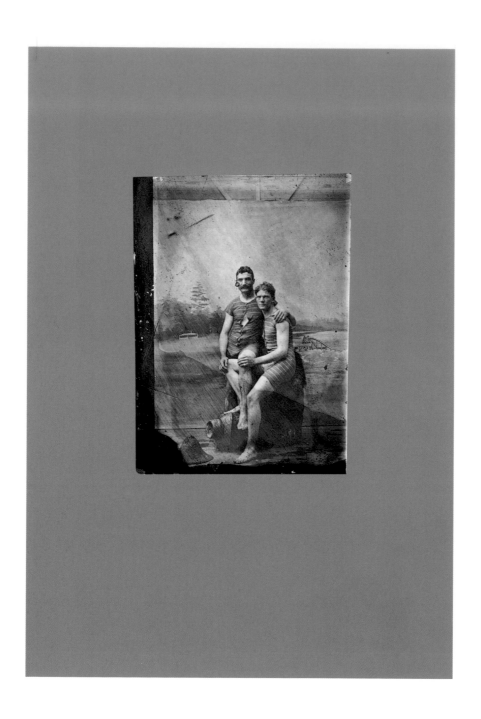

PHOTOGRAPHER UNKNOWN, SUBJECTS UNKNOWN, TINTYPE (3 × 2⁵/₈″), C. 1890

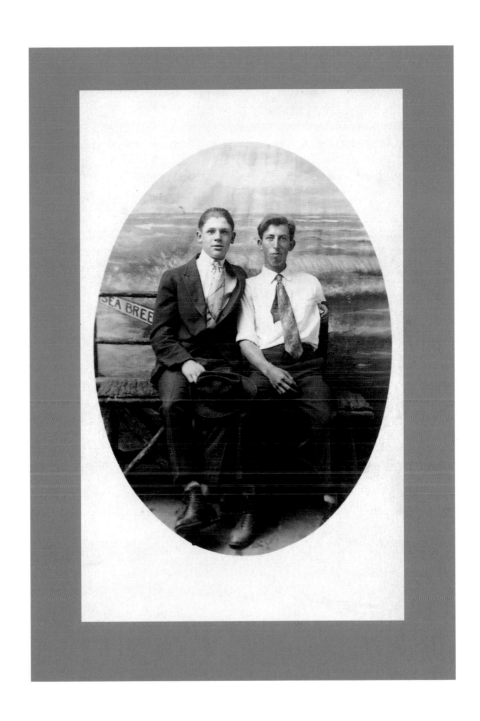

PHOTOGRAPHER UNKNOWN, SUBJECTS UNKNOWN, GELATIN SILVER PRINT, REAL PHOTO POSTCARD (5$\frac{1}{2}$ × 3$\frac{1}{2}$"), C. 1905

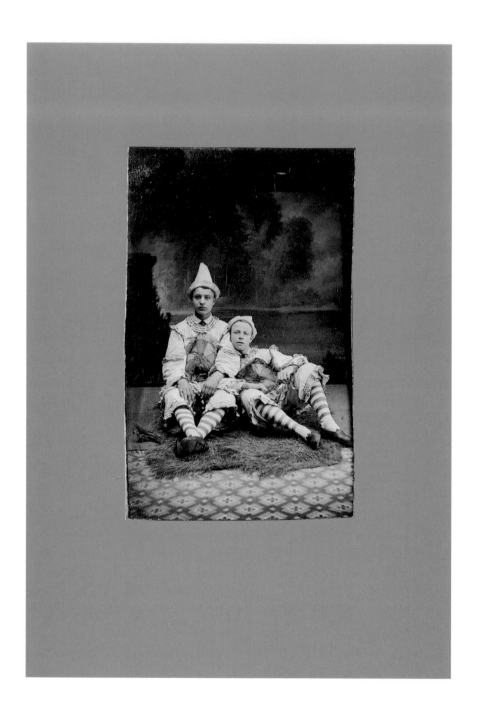

PHOTOGRAPHER UNKNOWN, SUBJECTS UNKNOWN, TINTYPE (3¾ × 2¼″), C. 1885

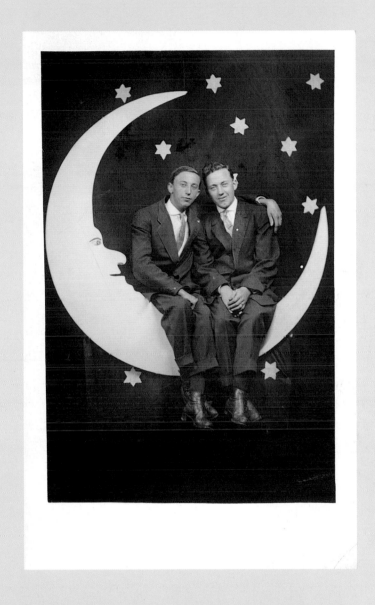

PHOTOGRAPHER UNKNOWN, HENRY SCHELBERGER AND ARTHUR ANDERSON, GELATIN SILVER PRINT, REAL PHOTO
POSTCARD (5½ × 3½"), C. 1915. INSCRIPTION ON VERSO READS: "HENRY SCHELBERGER & ARTHUR ANDERSON"

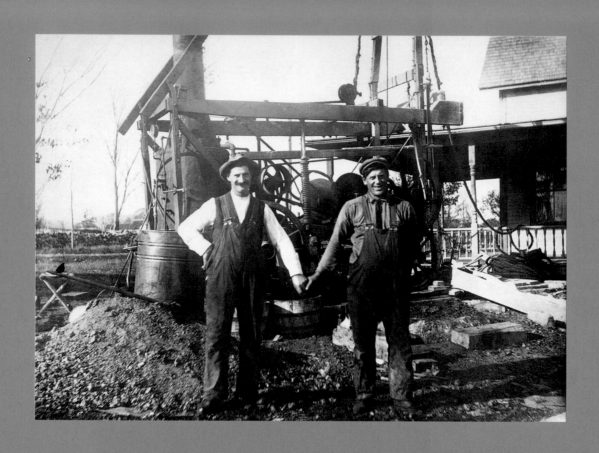

PHOTOGRAPHER UNKNOWN, SUBJECTS UNKNOWN, GELATIN SILVER PRINT, REAL PHOTO POSTCARD
($3\frac{1}{2} \times 5\frac{1}{2}$″), C. 1910. INSCRIPTION ON VERSO READS: "WELLDRILLING"

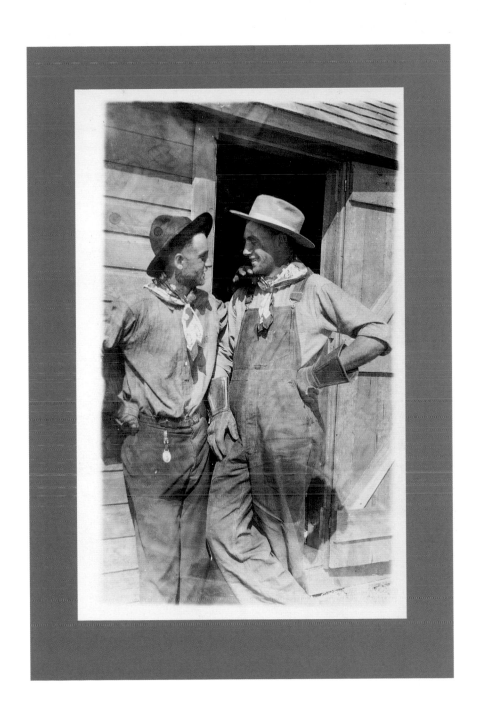

PHOTOGRAPHER UNKNOWN, SUBJECTS UNKNOWN, GELATIN SILVER PRINT, REAL PHOTO POSTCARD (5½ × 3½″), C. 1910

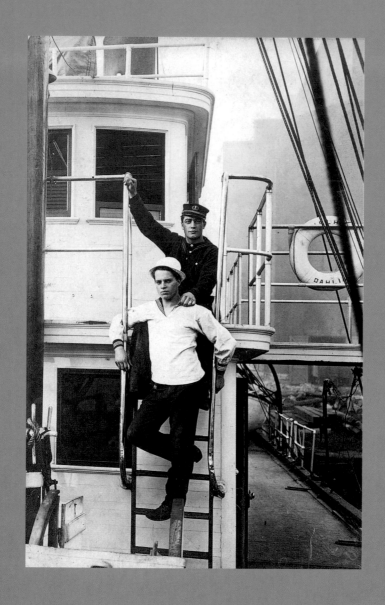

O. R. BAUMAN, SUBJECTS UNKNOWN, GELATIN SILVER PRINT, REAL PHOTO POSTCARD (5½ × 3½"), 1906. INSCRIPTION ON VERSO READS: "CHICAGO 9-23./DEAR COUSIN: MAY/FIND TIME SOON TO/WRITE YOU A LETTER/AT PRESENT THIS IS ALL I/CAN DO. BEST WISHES/TO ALL./J.K." POSTMARKED 1906. ADDRESSED TO MISS CLARA KOTTMAN/THORNTON/IOWA. BACKMARK ON VERSO READS: "THIS POST CARD IS A REAL PHOTOGRAPH MADE BY O. R. BAUMAN/[ILLEG.] CHICAGO"

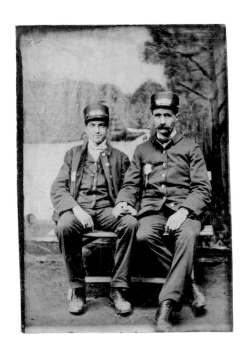

PHOTOGRAPHER UNKNOWN, SUBJECTS UNKNOWN, TINTYPE (3^1/$_2$ × 2^1/$_2$"), C. 1880

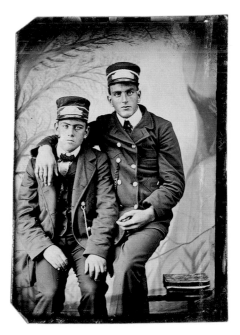

PHOTOGRAPHER UNKNOWN, SUBJECTS UNKNOWN, TINTYPE (3^1/$_2$ × 2^1/$_2$"), C. 1880

Related categories include military men, rangers, students, or members of business or sporting clubs. Sometimes the category may pertain to problems that arise in attempting to fix the meaning of more or less suggestive images about which so little can be known with any certainty. What is one to do, for example, with photographs in which the sitters resemble one another physically? Is it always a foregone conclusion (as skeptical observers so often insist) that the men in such photographs are blood relatives? Would the inclusion of such photographs necessarily undermine this book's implicit argument concerning the greater affectional freedom that men enjoyed before the end of World War I?

Such doubts help explain my mixed feelings on receiving a reproduction of a fine daguerreotype from the collector from Missouri. Identified on the velvet pad of the open case as the work of Willard, a photography studio on Market Street in Philadelphia, this crisp sixth-plate daguerreotype depicts two elegantly dressed men. The man on the left—clearly the elder—extends an arm around the shoulder of the more simply dressed fellow beside him who, in turn, rests a hand comfortably along the inner thigh of his stockier companion. My initial enthusiasm on seeing this photograph was soon tempered by recognizing their mutual resemblance. Could they be father and son? The collector also enclosed a copy of documentation that had accompanied the photograph when he bought it. In part, the documentation read: "A piece of paper behind the image has the names Henbraon Van Pelt and Ed Thomas." So, I concluded, they are not father and son. But could they still be uncle and nephew, or cousins perhaps? The collector volunteered to look into the census records for Philadelphia but found nothing definitive in relation to either name. I include the daguerreotype as a doubly cautionary reminder. Resemblance between affectionate men is no guarantee of their being—or of their not being—blood relations. As such, it signals, once again, the tension between what such photographs represent for the individual observer and what they may actually depict, underscoring the uncertainty that so resolutely adheres to them.

Within each thematic cluster of photographs, I arrange the individual images in a roughly chronological sequence. I'm curious to know whether this organization will reveal increasing or decreasing tenderness between men over the course of the nineteenth and early twentieth centuries, and, if so, when and under what conditions. Establishing such a sequence is possible in part because the history of male fashion provides

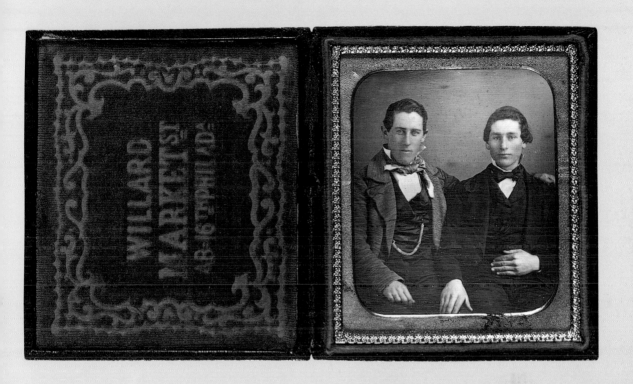

OLIVER H. WILLARD, HENBRAON VAN PELT AND ED. THOMAS, 1/6-PLATE DAGUERREOTYPE (3⁵/₈ × 3¹/₈″), C. 1855

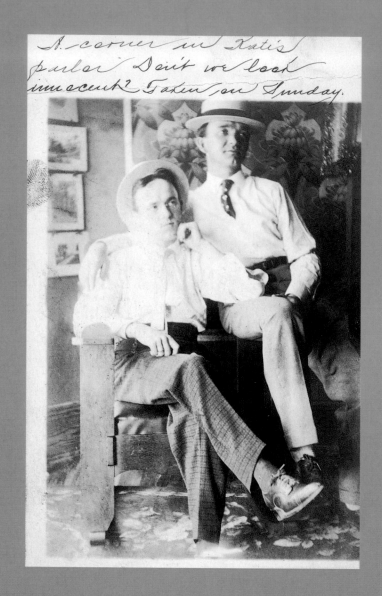

PHOTOGRAPHER UNKNOWN, SUBJECTS UNKNOWN, REAL PHOTO POSTCARD (5½ × 3½"), 1907. INSCRIPTION READS: "A CORNER IN KATE'S PARLOR. DON'T WE LOOK INNOCENT? TAKEN ON SUNDAY." ADDRESSED ON VERSO TO: "MISS M. SEGAN A.F.D. #1/BOX 20/LYNCHBURG VA." POSTMARKED: "JULY 8 11 AM CLEVELAND 1907"

some points of reference (though given the unpredictability of male style across class and geographical regions, these clues are not always reliable), and in part thanks to the progressive invention and abandonment of new methods of creating and commercially disseminating photographic imagery. It is widely understood that the earliest commercially viable photographs, daguerreotypes, show sitters posing uncomfortably as a result of having to remain perfectly still—not infrequently with the help of concealed head braces—for exposures lasting a minute or more. From this technical standpoint, one might therefore expect sitters to display greater spontaneity—if not necessarily greater intimacy—as exposure times grow shorter during the 1860s and 1870s. But from the vantage point of social history, one might expect a contrary development: that as the concepts of "sexual inversion" or "contrary sexual instinct" gained currency within bourgeois discourse, men would have been more reluctant to leave behind photographic traces of same-sex affection that could be taken for affection of the wrong kind.

To judge from the photographic evidence within this admittedly unscientific sample, the truth appears to be more complex. Many daguerreotypes contradict the cliché of the petrified sitter with deer-in-the-headlights eyes. More than a few show men interacting with an extraordinary ease, assuming all the most intimate poses that persist throughout the nineteenth- and early-twentieth-century history of photography. Such intimate and sometimes playful gestures persist through the age of the tintype into that of the "real photo" postcard before most of them disappear or get masked behind a tendency to humor and high-jinks, or are absorbed within the increasingly conventionalized, commercial markers of affectionate friendship.

A good number of the photographs recall specific works of art, as well as other forms of cultural imagery dating from before the invention of photography. From the iconographer's perspective, even the most prosaic or "natural" stance can bring apparently remote cultural precedents to mind. Looking at nineteenth-century photographs of men standing side by side with hands resting lightly on each other's shoulders, the iconographer is reminded of the classical composition known as the Three Graces. Countless men and women have posed like this, or have been positioned this way by photographers, presumably without anyone drawing the connection between this comfortable stance and the illustrious cultural pedigree of its high-art antecedent. This suggests the irrele-

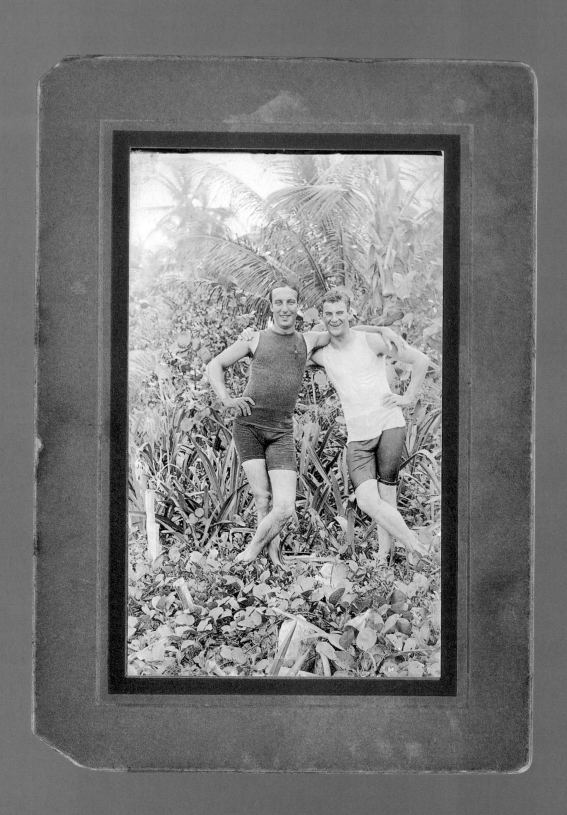

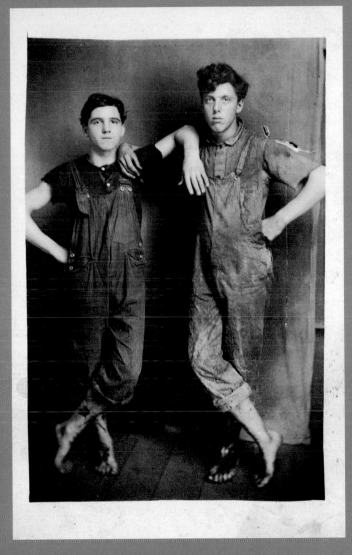

ABOVE: PHOTOGRAPHER UNKNOWN, SUBJECTS UNKNOWN, GELATIN SILVER PRINT,
REAL PHOTO POSTCARD (5½ × 3½"), C. 1905

OPPOSITE: E.VAL O'SHEA, SUBJECTS UNKNOWN, CABINET CARD (CARD: 7½ × 5¼"), 1910. INSCRIPTION ON VERSO
READS: "NOV.6–10/DEAREST MAE/THIS PICTURE WAS/TAKEN AT TORO POINT / BATHING BEACH IN THE / JUNGLES.
SOME CLASS. / FRANKIE." IMPRINT READS: "E.VAL O'SHEA,/CUITABLE [?]/CANAL ZONE"

vancy of the iconographer's method to understanding such old pictures of affectionate men. Although the correspondence between a given pose and its cultural legacy may be fortuitous, that does not necessarily render it meaningless. Thus, during the Renaissance, the arrangement of three idealized female nudes standing side by side linked by hands resting on each other's shoulders was understood to symbolize *Amitias* (friendship). *Amitias* was itself considered "a subsidiary virtue under the cardinal virtue Justitia."[75] As a conceptualization of friendship, "Amitias" therefore contributed to the exalted social status that friendship would retain throughout the eighteenth and into the nineteenth centuries.

The historian Michael Lynch has identified three stages in the historical transformation of social attitudes toward same-sex affection: first, the "friendship tradition" of the late eighteenth and early nineteenth centuries; second, the mid-nineteenth-century conception of comradely love, as promoted by Walt Whitman; third, the late-nineteenth-century identification of same-sex affection with homosexuality. Phrenological speculations regarding the "organs" of Adhesiveness and Amativeness— the portions of the brain believed to predispose an individual to friendship and sensuality, respectively—contributed to the conceptual transformation of affectionate male-male relations from idealized friendship to comradeship to homosexuality. Some phrenologists were more than mildly interested in the iconography of Adhesiveness. George Combe (1784–1858), a Scottish-born lawyer and immensely influential phrenologist, believed in the "doctrine about natural language." That is to say, he looked to cultural imagery—past and present—for physical expressions of Adhesiveness. Such a doctrine of a natural language is consistent with the contemporaneous photographs that the French neuropathologist Jean-Martin Charcot had taken of his female patients at La Salpêtrière in Paris in his attempt to locate in their facial expressions external evidence of the psychopathological conditions that had led to their confinement. When applied to art history, the doctrine of "natural language" relates to the "natural" body language that ensures the widespread legibility of certain poses, gestures, and expressions throughout the history of figurative art. As phrenologists turned to art historical representations, they profited from the conventional dependence of Western artists on the close study of the human figure. In this way, the artistic distillation of conventional poses produced results that were not only visually pleasing but universally legible as evidence of the shared choreography of everyday bodily experience. "Look at the pictures of Castor and Pollux," Combe wrote of the mythological twin sons of Leda (and the brothers of Helen) who were famed for their fraternal affection, "in which the one stands with his arm passed over the shoulder of the other, the two heads touching at a point a little behind and above the ear." Combe further proposed that if one were to place "any two persons, no matter although of the same sex, in both of whom the organs of Adhesiveness are large, in this position . . . you will soon discover whether or not this is the natural attitude of attachment."[76]

Phrenologists identified the point on the cranium "a little behind and above the ear" as the physiological site of Adhesiveness. Had Combe been able to study nineteenth- and early-twentieth-century photographs of American men, he would probably have seized on one frequently recurring pose as proof that in the United States highly developed organs of Adhesiveness were virtually epidemic. Many photographs survive that attest to the popularity of this charming pose, in which men are seen in tight close-ups with their heads inclined so that they touch above, and often a little behind, the ear. This "adhesive" pose dates back to the second half of the 1850s, to the period of the earliest tintypes, and extends forward into twentieth-century paper prints by studio photographers, and even to the poses that friends hurriedly assume inside the close quarters of mid-twentieth-century photomats. According to Combe's tautological reasoning, the prevalence of the adhesive pose would prove not only that the sitters were fond of each other but that they must have possessed organs of Adhesiveness large enough to effect an irresistible tug of magnetic attraction from the head of one man to the other's. Combe implied the existence of just such a gravitational pull when he described children who "put their arms around each other's necks, and place their heads together, bringing the organ of Adhesiveness in each into contact with the same organ in the other." Phrenologists thus exploited representations of such a "natural attitude of attachment" to lend support to their argument about the existence and power of the organ of Adhesiveness.[77]

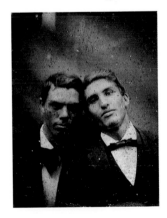

PHOTOGRAPHER UNKNOWN, SUBJECTS UNKNOWN, GEM TINTYPE (1 × ¾"), C. 1885

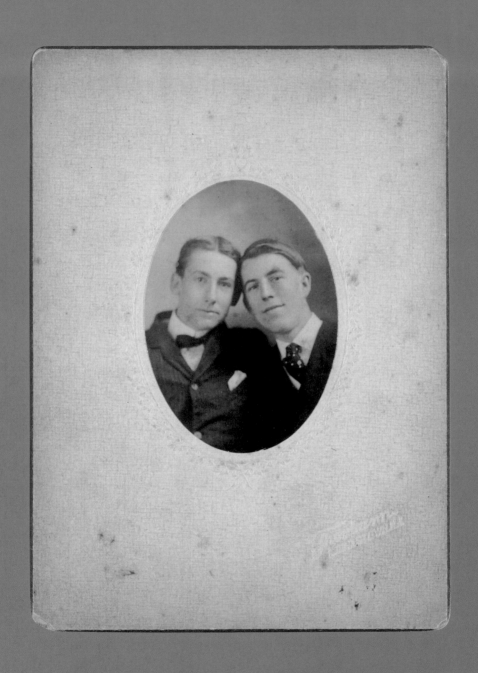

THORBURN, CLIFFORD STULK (?) AND RAYMOND WICKOFF, CABINET CARD (CARD: 6¹/₂ × 4¹/₄"), C. 1900. INSCRIPTION ON VERSO READS: "CLIFFORD STULK (?). / RAYMOND WICKOFF." BACKMARK ON VERSO READS: "THORBURN/HIGHTSTOWN, N.J."

* * *

Among the more striking gestures that nineteenth-century American men employed to register their mutual affection was holding hands. In some of these photographs, the men also lean together, their bodies forming a loosely triangular composition that recalls one of the icons that phrenologists used to denote the organ of Adhesiveness in the phrenological maps of the human head that were widely disseminated by Fowler and Wells. In such diagrams the head, seen in profile, is subdivided into its various phrenological quadrants, each one labeled by a tattoo-like icon of its own. Lynch reports that the icon signaling Adhesiveness shows "two young women holding hands, their heads tilted together so that, presumably, their adhesive organs were as close as possible." He also notes a later nineteenth-century sketch by the Fowler organization in which the organ of Adhesiveness is symbolized by a drawing of two men, "their arms are linked in a distinct male friendship pose."[78]

Such phrenological icons and the poses of affectionate men that resemble them are both reminiscent of an earlier nineteenth-century allegory of friendship and love, a well-known painting by the German artist Philip Overbeck (1789–1869). Entitled *Italia und Germania* (1811–29), the painting shows two young women—one blonde, the other brunette—seated before a landscape that contains architectural details evocative of appropriately Mediterranean or Northern Gothic traditions. The young women lean together to form a triangular composition, their heads drawn together and apparently touching. The figure symbolizing Germany leans forward to take the right hand of her more timid Mediterranean friend in her own. Overbeck was a dissident student at the Vienna Academy in 1809 when he joined with his friend and colleague Franz Pforr (1788–1812) in resurrecting the idea of the medieval artists' guild. Together they founded an artists' organization that they named the Brotherhood of St. Luke. Artists affiliated with the Brotherhood became better known as the Nazarenes, a possibly derogatory nickname that was applied to them after its participants took vows of chastity and poverty, let their hair grow long, and moved into cells in the deconsecrated monastery of Sant'Isidoro in Rome. There they set about studying early Renaissance art as assiduously as they had the art of Northern Renaissance masters such as Albrecht Dürer in the hopes of restoring to European painting the clarity and simplicity that Baroque art

141

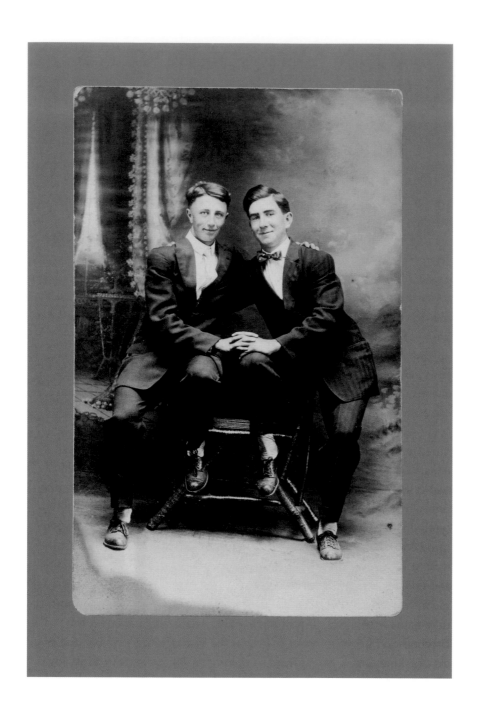

PHOTOGRAPHER UNKNOWN, SUBJECTS UNKNOWN, GELATIN SILVER PRINT, REAL PHOTO POSTCARD
(5½ × 3½"), C. 1905. INSCRIPTION ON VERSO READS: "SAM SHIMP/GEORGE TROOP"

had clouded. The art historian Robert Rosenblum has written that the symbolism of *Italia und Germania* is so private an invention that it remains disturbing and elusive, and speculates that this elusiveness might be due to the fact that "the union of these two brides, as Overbeck called them, probably projects unconsciously the passionate friendship between the two founders of the Nazarenes."[79] Unconscious or not, this painting was not the only work by a member of the Nazarene brotherhood that testified to the passionate friendships that flourished among them. Overbeck and his colleagues were also in the habit of drawing and painting portraits of themselves and of each other, and of exchanging these works as keepsakes and tokens of affection. In this way, they anticipated the "pledge of friendship" that later would be commercialized and popularized by photography.

While the pairs of men who sat together before the camera in culturally significant poses were in all likelihood unaware of that fact, there is reason to believe that the photographers who arranged the sitters were more concerned about such matters. In *The Camera and the Pencil*, M. A. Root recommended the study of Western art as a means of improving the overall quality of American photography in the nineteenth century. In addition to providing technical advice, Root quoted passages on aesthetics from the writings of Sir Joshua Reynolds. Among other key monuments of Western art, he urged that photographers study "the engravings of Da Vinci's 'Lord's Supper,'" that they note "how much is expressed by the arrangement and posture of each figure; and most of all, by each face, in which one may almost read the thoughts agitated within, and the words about to break forth."[80]

In a development that paralleled the contemporaneous claim of phrenologists to find the particularities of individual character inscribed on the surface of an individual's head, Root prescribed specific poses to communicate specific meanings.

If in the same picture two persons are to be portrayed, both sitting, the one should be represented as leaning lightly on the other's chair, and the face of each should be turned partly towards the other, as if a conversation was going on. Or they may be placed opposite to each other at a table, the one with the right and the other with the left arm resting thereon, and the persons of both gently bending towards each other, as though they were conversing; or one may be seated, while the other stands nigh him, leaning familiarly on the latter's shoulder or chair back.[81]

Such advice had far-reaching effects on photographic practice among amateurs as well as professionals. Root's advice that one man sit while the other stand nearby with a hand "familiarly" on his shoulder or chair back reflects in only the most limited way the broad social acceptance of physical demonstrations of affection between men. Yet throughout the nineteenth century this pose dominates photographs of friends—as well as of husbands and wives. It depicts "affection" in a codified and relatively inexpressive way, yielding a generic standard among photographs of more or less affectionate pairs.

So codified did this pose become that sitting and standing were eventually identifiable as gendered positions. As popularized in photographs of married couples, the seated position was habitually reserved for the man, while the woman stood attentively and deferentially behind him and to his side. This convention was often reiterated in images of men together. This is evident, for example, in several photographs of Whitman that were taken over a twenty-year span in the company of various young comrades, including Peter Doyle, William Stafford, Bill Ducket, and Warren Fritzinger. In each of these portraits the poet is seated in the authoritative, masculine position, while his younger friend stands like an attendant slightly behind and to his side. In these photographs, authority as well as age come before beauty.

There are also anonymous photographs in which the same gender coding of the two positions is so vividly demonstrated as to suggest a possibly satirical, or anyway playful, intent. Consider the cabinet card shot by Crowell of Waltham, Massachusetts, in which a swarthy, mustachioed young man in a sailor suit sits with his legs comfortably crossed in the company of a burly companion who occupies the feminine position standing behind and to his side in full feminine drag. As if to underscore the element of role-playing that is already explicit in this image of two men in costume (were they going to a masked ball? a carnival?), each holds a mask—the sailor's a strikingly reflexive representation of his own mustachioed face painted on what appears to be gauze, the burly maiden's an unarticulated rectangle of white cotton with slits cut out for eyes.

In a similar photograph by D. J. Wilkes of Baltimore, each figure's costume corresponds with the traditionally masculine (sitting) and feminine (standing) arrangement, but other aspects of each participant raise unsettling doubts about the gender of both. Thus the standing figure, sporting a full-skirted damask gown with lace collar and cuffs, sports an

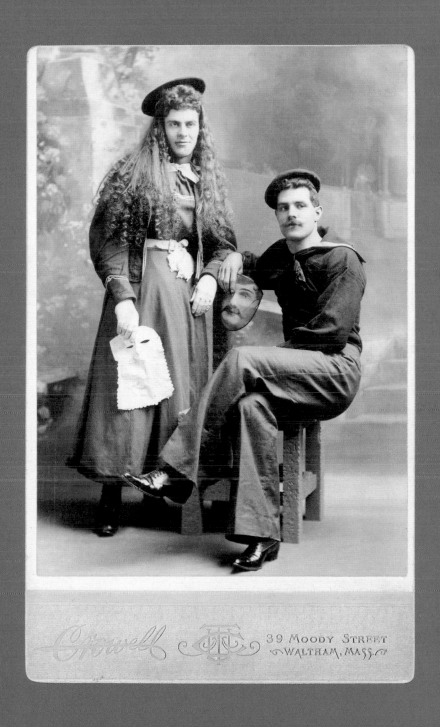

UAH T. CROWELL, SUBJECTS UNKNOWN, CABINET CARD (OVERALL: 6⅝ × 4⅛"), C. 1897–98.
IMPRINT READS: "U. T. CROWELL, 39 MOODY STREET/ WALTHAM, MASS."

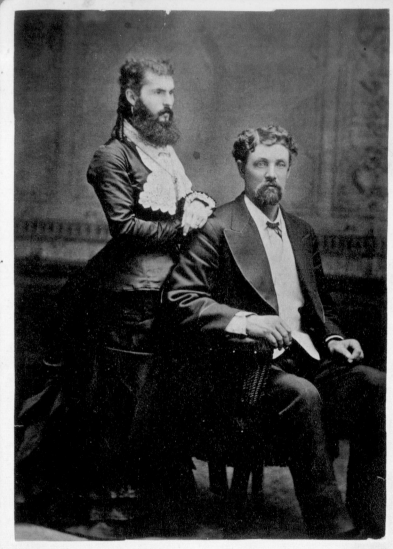

CABINET PORTRAIT.

D. J. WILKES,
Photographer,

125 W. Baltimore St.
Baltimore, Md.

D. J. WILKES, SUBJECTS UNKNOWN, CABINET CARD (6½ × 4¼"), C. 1885. IMPRINT READS:
"CABINET PORTRAIT/ D. J. WILKES,/ PHOTOGRAPHER,/ 125 W. BALTIMORE ST./ BALTIMORE, MD."

ample beard. The mustache and goatee of the seated figure seem curiously at odds with his smooth skin, fair eyes, and fine hair; and with the way that his body fairly swims inside a loose-fitting dinner jacket with broad lapels, white vest, shirt, and tie. There are qualities about each figure that don't quite add up convincingly to the conclusion that one quickly draws from the sight of the cabinet card showing the sailor and his beefy "maiden": that both are men in, respectively, masculine and feminine drag. Rather than seeming to be the private memento of two men's unusually elaborate and playful preparations for a night on the town, Wilkes's photograph suggests the commercial depiction of two "bearded ladies" intended for sale in the burgeoning marketplace for photographic novelties. Although its intended function remains unknown, the capacity of this image to induce uneasiness in the minds of observers, then and now, depends in part on the willingness of the androgynous pair to occupy the positions that were prescribed as gendered by nineteenth-century conventions of portrait photography.

★   ★   ★

On Thursday, January 17, 1889, Horace Traubel paid one of his many visits to Walt Whitman at the poet's Camden home. Traubel records that on this occasion he found the poet engaged in "looking up old portraits." Traubel asked Whitman how it was that he seemed to "come naturally by good photos," to which Whitman replied: "I don't fix up when I go to have a picture taken." Traubel then ventured that it would be a good idea if "we might some day have a W. gallery—a book giving W. portraits—lots—all." The mention of such a "gallery" then prompted the aging poet to recall a conversation he had had with Mathew Brady in more youthful times. "We had many a talk together," he reminisced, "the point was, how much better it would often be, rather than having a lot of contradictory records by witnesses or historians—say of Caesar, Socrates, Epictetus, others—if we could have three or four or half a dozen portraits—very accurate—of the men: that would be history—the best history—a history from which there could be no appeal."[82] From the postmodern perspective, in which photography's claim to unassailable, objective truth is considered, at best, naive, Whitman's equation

147

of portrait photographs with "the best history" can seem preposterous, if not downright perverse—especially if one considers the case of Whitman himself. For notwithstanding the fact that he was among the most frequently and skillfully photographed Americans of his day, Whitman has remained a stubbornly enigmatic figure—particularly when it comes to the matter of his sexuality. Despite a wealth of photographic testimony, Whitman is the object of impassioned and always "contradictory records" by both witnesses and historians.

Whitman's assertion seems especially strange in light of one of the photographs he posed for. Shortly after the end of the Civil War, Whitman and his "rebel soldier friend," Peter Doyle, paid a visit to the studio of the photographer Moses P. Rice in Washington, D.C. During that visit, Rice created two albumen photographs of the two men. In one, Doyle stands behind and to the side of the seated Whitman, resting a hand "familiarly" on the poet's shoulder as Whitman looks up to his younger friend. More remarkable is the second photograph in which the two men, sporting jaunty hats, gaze into each other's eyes while seated facing one another in opposing wooden chairs. One day before Whitman recalled his encounter with Brady and made his assertion about photography being the best history, Traubel jotted down his impressions on seeing the picture that day: "Doyle has a sickly smile on his face: W. lovingly serene: the two looking stagily at each other, almost sheepishly." Traubel also noted Whitman's reaction to seeing the photograph again (he "laughed heartily the instant I put my hands on it"), as well as that of Whitman's friend and literary executor Thomas Harned. Traubel reports: "Harned mimicked Doyle, W. retorting: 'Never mind, the expression on my face atones for all that is lacking in his. What do I look like there? Is it seriosity?' Harned suggested: 'Fondness, and Doyle should be a girl.'"

But perhaps photography's incapacity to settle the matter of Whitman's sexuality is precisely what suited the poet's intentions. Traubel's visits with Whitman date from the period late in the poet's life when he was engaged in what the historian David Reynolds has called the "mass destruction of private documents . . . connected to a suppression of evidence about his relations with men." It was also at that time that Whitman "exercised self-censorship in his diaries, especially in the 1870 Doyle passage, in which he changed pronouns and used a numerical code to cloak Doyle's identity."[83] In 1890, Whitman also saw fit to reply to the numerous, hitherto unanswered letters that the British writer

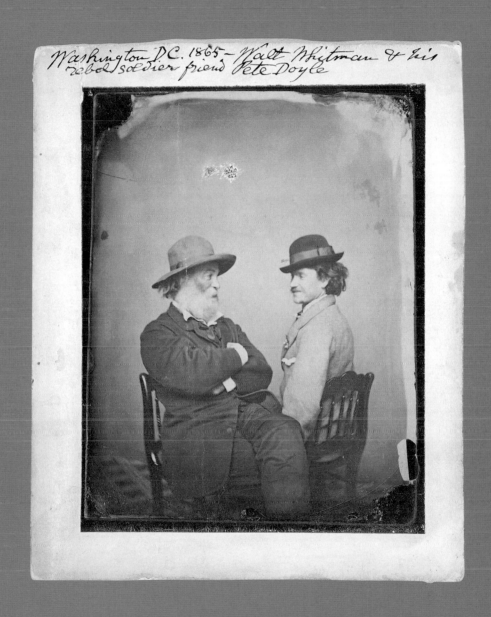

MOSES P. RICE, WALT WHITMAN AND PETER DOYLE, ALBUMEN PRINT (5⅝ × 4½"), 1865. INSCRIPTION ON PAPER
MOUNT READS: "WASHINGTON D.C. 1865—WALT WHITMAN & HIS/REBEL SOLDIER FRIEND PETER DOYLE"

John Addington Symonds had mailed him requesting clarification regarding the meaning of "Calamus." Not only did Whitman rebuke Symonds for "morbid inferences," he also considered it appropriate in this context to brag about having sired six children—an assertion that Reynolds judges "almost certainly a lie." Even in the unlikely case that Whitman's claim of paternity were truthful, it would not have impressed Symonds, who was himself both homosexual, a married man, and a father. Reynolds has argued that Whitman's reaction to Symonds's inquiries were the product of the poet's combined incapacity and unwillingness to assimilate his fluid conception of comradely love to the imminent petrification of human affections by a European discourse that classified human beings as either heterosexual or homosexual. Whitman may have been confused "about 'Calamus' and his own sexual self," Reynolds writes, "but these confusions emerged from the American working-class culture of comrades and romantic friends that had shaped him."[84]

There may be another vantage point from which it is possible to agree with Whitman's estimation of photographic portraits as "the best history—a history from which there could be no appeal." Such a perspective would depend on the incapacity, especially of the undocumented and anonymous photograph, to communicate a fixed meaning. The history from which there can be no appeal is the mute, vivid, visual record of something or someone who was but no longer is. In their irresolvable ambiguity, the anonymous portraits of comrades and romantic friends that fill the pages of this book cannot ultimately be enlisted as incontrovertible evidence of a gay past; but neither, by the same token, can they be taken as proof that such a past did not exist. We are left, then, with uncertainty, with that blend of desire and doubt that transports the observer to conduct research that itself leads back to uncertainty. In their elusiveness, their resistance to naming and categorization, such photographs become their own best poetic evidence of the fluidity that marked the relations they reveal yet cannot prove.

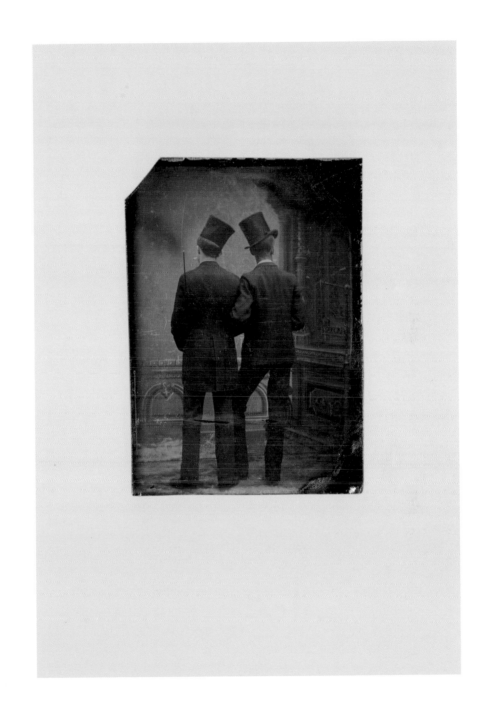

PHOTOGRAPHER UNKNOWN, SUBJECTS UNKNOWN, TINTYPE (3$\frac{1}{2}$ × 2$\frac{3}{8}$ "), C. 1880

NOTES

★

1. Neil Bartlett, *Who Was That Man? A Present for Mr. Oscar Wilde* (London: Serpent's Tail Press, 1985), 129.

2. Adam Phillips, *On Flirtation: Psychoanalytic Essays on the Uncommitted Life* (Cambridge, Mass.: Harvard University Press, 1994), xvii, xix. My thanks to Julie Ault for bringing Phillips's work to my attention.

3. Sam Howe Verhovek, "Cattle Barons of Texas Yore Accused of Epic Land Grab," *New York Times*, July 14, 1997, A1, A12.

4. "Of the Terrible Doubt of Appearances," in Walt Whitman, *Leaves of Grass* (New York: The Modern Library, 1993), 152.

5. Anthony Rotundo, "Romantic Friendship: Male Intimacy and Middle-Class Youth in the Northern United States, 1800–1900," *Journal of Social History* 23, no.1 (1989), 14.

6. For an enlightening discussion of male homosexuality as viewed by Freud and his followers, see Kenneth Lewes, *The Psychoanalytic Theory of Male Homosexuality* (New York: Simon and Schuster, 1988).

7. This point may well be the most important, and least troubling, contribution to be found in Daniel Harris's collection of essays, *The Rise and Fall of Gay Culture* (New York: Hyperion, 1997).

8. See John D'Emilio, *Sexual Politics, Sexual Communities: The Making of a Homosexual Minority in the United States, 1940-1970* (Chicago: University of Chicago Press, 1983).

9. Perhaps the most spectacular demonstration of such historical hubris is the corporate-sponsored "restoration" of the Sistine Chapel in Rome. I am not interested in whether or not this Herculean effort has "restored" Michelangelo's frescoes to anything approaching their condition in the artist's day. That does not seem a question that anyone lacking a time machine can reasonably hope to answer. Far more interesting is the underlying attitude that modern technologies can somehow cleanse the material consequences of a half millennium, and the accompanying idea that this is a *historical* thing to do—as if the Renaissance could be made more immediate to the conditions of life at the end of the twentieth century. That this rehabilitation has occurred during Pope John Paul II's reassertion of papal authority, with funding from a Japanese film company, speaks volumes about the relationship between such spectacular acts of historical and cultural reclamation and the institutions that find such actions desirable.

10. For this, and subsequent quotations, see Caroll Smith-Rosenberg, "The Female World of Love and Ritual: Relations between Women in Nineteenth-Century America," in *Disorderly Conduct: Visions of Gender in Victorian America* (New York: Alfred A. Knopf, 1985), 53–76. Among other contributions to the literature on this subject are: John D'Emilio and Estelle B. Freedman, *Intimate Matters: A History of Sexuality in America* (New York: Harper & Row, Publishers, 1988); Lilian Faderman, *Surpassing the Love of Men: Romantic Friendship and Love Between Women from the Renaissance to the Present* (New York: William Morrow and Co., 1981); Peter Gay, *The Tender Passion*, vol. 2 of *The Bourgeois Experience: Victoria to Freud* (New York: Oxford University Press, 1986); Jonathan Ned Katz, *Gay American History: Lesbians and Gay Men in the USA* (New York: Thomas Crowell, 1976); and *The Invention of Heterosexuality* (New York: Dutton Books, 1995); Michael Lynch, "'Here is Adhesiveness': From Friendship to Homosexuality," *Victorian Studies* 85 (autumn 1985), 67–96; and Anthony Rotundo, "Romantic Friendship: Male Intimacy and Middle-Class Youth in the Northern United States, 1800-1900," *Journal of Social History* 23, no.1 (1989), 1–25.

11. Alexis de Tocqueville, *Democracy in America* (New York, Anchor Books, 1969), 601.

12. See D'Emilio and Freedman, 129.

13. Smith-Rosenberg, 76.

14. The Journal of Albert Dodd resides among the Albert Dodd Papers, Yale University Library, Manuscript and Archives. The source for my quotations from it is Gay, 206–11.

15. Whitman, quoted in D'Emilio and Freedman, 127.

16. Rotundo, 2.

17. Ibid., 1, 3.

18. Quoted in Katz, *Gay American History*, 459.

19. Rotundo, 9.

20. See Michel Foucault, *The History of Sexuality*, vol. 1 (New York: Vintage Books, 1980); David Halperin, *One Hundred Years of Homosexuality* (New York: Routledge, 1990); and Jonathan Ned Katz, *The Invention of Heterosexuality* (New York: Dutton, 1995).

21. See George Chauncey, *Gay New York: Gender, Urban Culture, and the Making of the Gay Male World, 1890–1940* (New York: Basic Books, 1994), 403, note 50.

22. Rotundo, 12–14.

23. Donald Yacavone, "Abolitionists and the 'Language of Fraternal Love,'" in Mark C. Carnes and Clyde Griffen, eds. *Meanings for Manhood: Constructions of Masculinity in Victorian America* (Chicago: University of Chicago Press, 1990), 89.

24. Ibid., 90–93.

25. Gay, 238.

26. Ibid., 210.

27. Yacavone, 94.

28. Determined to pin down the ultimate meaning of young Daniel Webster's letter to his "Dearly Beloved" Hervey Bingham, in which Webster conjured a future in which "we will yoke together again; your little bed is just wide enough," Rotundo concludes: "That playful statement may have been made *in total innocence.* The most useful means of understanding Webster's suggestion, though, is one that recognizes bed partners as a common custom of the time, even as it concedes more intimate possibilities for two men who sleep together" (italics added). I am not as concerned with the accuracy or inaccuracy of Rotundo's statement, nor even with his methodology, as with the compulsion to make sense of these nineteenth-century facts in terms of twentieth-century dichotomies. Rotundo, 3–4, 11.

29. Among the scarce documentation that proves what went on in bed between American men in the nineteenth century could well have been genital sex is one letter from 1826, which includes the following: "I feel some inclination to learn whether you yet sleep in your Shirt-tail, and whether you yet have the extravagant delight of poking and punching a writhing Bedfellow with your long fleshen pole—the exquisite touches of which I have often had the honor of feeling?" See "'Writhing Bedfellows' in Antebellum South Carolina: Historical Interpretation and the Politics of Evidence," in Martin Duberman, ed., *About Time: Exploring the Gay Past* (New York: Meridian Books, 1991), 5.

30. Tocqueville, quoted in Alan Trachtenberg, *Reading American Photographs: Images as History, Mathew Brady to Walker Evans* (New York: Hill and Wang, 1989), 43.

31. Clark, quoted in Bruce Laurie, *Artisans into Workers: Labor in Nineteenth-Century America* (Urbana: University of Illinois Press, 1997), 36. Laurie adds that the social relations of artisanal production were no panacea. "As early as the 1780s urban masters slighted their moral and educative obligations to apprentices even as they continued to provide them with food and shelter. They took on trainees without the slightest intention of imparting the subtleties of their craft and treated them solely as sources of cheap labor. For their part, apprentices were often restive, not afraid to run off with only a rudimentary knowledge of their calling."

32. Ibid., 40.

33. Ibid., 41.

34. Oliver Wendell Holmes, "Doings of the Sunbeam," *Atlantic Monthly* 12 (July 1863): 2.

35. Alan Trachtenberg, "Albums of War: On Reading Civil War Photographs," *Representations* 9 (winter 1985): 11.

36. Horace Greeley quoted in Heinz K. Henisch, Bridget A. Henisch, *The Photographic Experience,*

1839–1914: Images and Attitudes (University Park, Pa.: The Pennsylvania State University Press, 1994), 165.

37. Root identified the second function for portrait photography, to borrow Trachtenberg's term, as emulative: "But not alone our near and dear are thus kept with us; the great and the good, the heroes, saints, and sages of all lands and all eras are, by these life-like 'presentments,' brought within the constant purview of the young, the middle-aged, and the old." In other words, photographs of the "great and the good" served an educational function, providing figures of greatness for Americans to emulate. See Marcus Aurelius Root, *The Camera and the Pencil, or, the Heliographic Art* (1864; Reprint: Helios, 1971), 26–27. In identifying distinctly private and public functions for photographic portraiture—the first sentimental, the second potentially edifying—Root provides evidence of photography's participation in the modern partition of nineteenth-century life into opposing private and public spheres.

38. "Mass transiency remains the most striking finding to emerge from quantitative studies of nineteenth-century North America. . . . On a more general level, the degree to which the population around them swirled and the frequency with which they themselves moved helped shape the way in which people viewed their world. Friendships were difficult to maintain; ties to individuals were tenuous." See Michael B. Katz, Michael J. Doucet, and Mark J. Stern, *The Social Organization of Early Industrial Capitalism* (Cambridge, Mass.: Harvard University Press, 1982), 129.

39. Trachtenberg, "Albums of War: On Reading Civil War Photographs," 5.

40. Quoted in Drew Johnson and Marcia Eymann, eds. *Silver and Gold: Cased Images of the California Gold Rush* (Iowa City: University of Iowa Press, 1998), 207.

41. See Susan Lee Johnson, "Bulls, Bears, and Dancing Boys: Race, Gender, and Leisure in the California Gold Rush," *Radical History Review* no. 60 (1994): 23. I am grateful to Gary Kurutz of the State Library of California who brought this essay to my attention.

42. Michael Kimmel, *Manhood in America: A Cultural History* (New York: The Free Press, 1996), 55.

43. Mary Ryan, *Cradle of the Middle Class: The Family in Oneida County, New York, 1790–1865* (Cambridge: Cambridge University Press, 1981), 106. On the taste for facial hair, see Dwight Robinson, "Fashions in Shaving and Trimming the Beard: The Men of the *Illustrated London News*, 1842–1972," *American Journal of Sociology* 81, no. 5 (1976): 1136ff.

44. James M. McPherson, *For Cause and Comrades: Why Men Fought in the Civil War* (New York: Oxford University Press, 1997), 85–87.

45. Ibid., 55, 56.

46. Whitman, quoted in David Reynolds, *Walt Whitman's America* (New York: Alfred A. Knopf, Inc., 1995), 429.

47. See *Specimen Days by Walt Whitman* (Boston: David R. Godine, 1971), 45.

48. Five of these cartes-de-visite are reproduced in ibid., 50–52.

49. Quoted in Robert Taft, *Photography and the American Scene: A Social History, 1839–1889* (New York: Dover Publications, Inc., 1938), 148.

50. Ibid., 160.

51. See William S. Johnson, *Nineteenth-Century Photography: An Annotated Bibliography, 1839–1879* (Boston: G. K. Hall & Co., 1990), 398–99.

52. Harwood, quoted in Mark C. Carnes, *Secret Ritual and Manhood in Victorian America* (New Haven: Yale University Press, 1989), 1. The description of fraternal rituals that follows derives from the far more extensive and detailed accounts in Carnes's book.

53. Kimmel, 56.

54. Katz, *Gay American History*, 673.

55. On the execution of homosexuals, whether by public incineration (hence: "faggot") or by hanging, which British law prescribed from 1533 and well into the era of Wordsworth, Coleridge, Byron, Shelly, and Keats, see Louis Crompton, *Byron and Greek Love: Homophobia in 19th-Century England* (Berkeley: University of California Press, 1985), 12–62.

56. D'Emilio and Freedman, 122.

57. Philip Callow, *From Noon to Starry Night: A Life of Walt Whitman* (Chicago: Ivan R. Dee, Publisher, 1992), 189.

58. O. S. Fowler, *Amativeness* (New York, 1856), n.p.

59. According to David Reynolds, Peter Doyle "came closer than anyone else to being the love of his life." See Reynolds, 487.

60. Reynolds compares the catechistic fervor of Whitman's diary entry—notably its hysterical deployment of the upper case—with affirmations such as those that Fowler prescribed for individuals whose adhesiveness, and especially whose amativeness, is "disproportionate." Fowler proposed: "Total ABSTINENCE IS LIFE . . . . INDULGENCE IS A TRIPLE THREAT. Resolution: Determination to stop NOW AND FOREVER." See Reynolds, 249–50.

61. Caroll Smith-Rosenberg, "Sex as Symbol in Victorian Purity," *American Journal of Sociology* 84, Supplement (1978): 220.

62. Using R. T. Trall's tract as an example, Smith-Rosenberg has noted the use of masturbation as code for homosexuality. See ibid., 225–26.

63. Gay, 205.

64. See Reynolds, 539–40.

65. Labouchère Amendment quoted in Jeffrey Weeks, *Coming Out: Homosexual Politics in Britain from the Nineteenth Century to the Present* (London: Quartet Book Limited, 1977), 14.

66. Regarding Symonds' "apologia," and his appeal to Whitman, see Gay, 228–29, 248.

67. Stead, quoted in Weeks, 21.

68. Of the legislative initiatives related to male same-sex sexuality which swept Prussia, Great Britain, and Denmark, Peter Gay has observed: "Indeed, lessening the stringency of penalties against sodomy and related offenses only increased the inclination of authorities to prosecute and of juries to convict." Gay, 220ff.

69. See Eve Kosofsky Sedgwick, *Between Men: English Literature and Male Homosocial Desire* (New York: Columbia University Press, 1985).

70. See Reynolds, 461, 569.

71. See Chauncey, 57, 385, note 2.

72. Many thanks to Deborah Bright for alerting me to the historical correspondence between the popularization of the snapshot and the historical construction of normative heterosexuality. See Michel Foucault, *Discipline and Punish: The Birth of the Prison*, trans. Alan Sheridan (New York: Vintage Books, 1979).

73. See Pat Barker, *The Eye in the Door* (New York: Plume, 1995), 156, 278–80.

74. See Randy Shilts, *Conduct Unbecoming: Gays and Lesbians in the U.S. Military* (New York: Ballantine Books, 1993), 15–16.

75. See Mab van Lohuizen-Mulder, *Raphael's Images of Justice, Humanity, Friendship: A Mirror of Princes for Scipione Borghese* (Wassenaar: Miranda, 1977), 101.

76. See Lynch, 76. I have unfortunately been unable to locate the representations of Castor and Pollux to which Combe refers.

77. Ibid.

78. Ibid., 85.

79. Robert Rosenblum, *19th-Century Art* (New York: Harry N. Abrams, 1984), 82–84.

80. Root, 99.

81. Ibid., 107.

82. Horace Traubel, *With Walt Whitman in Camden*, vol. 3 (New York: Mitchell Kennerly, 1914), 542–543, 553.

83. Reynolds, 577.

84. Ibid., 397.

INDEX

★

Page numbers in *italics* refer to illustrations

Emerson, Ralph Waldo, 34; and Martin Gay, 52, 55
Epictetus (Greek philosopher), 147
Eye in the Door, The (Barker), 118

factories: and effect on artisanal way of life, 68–70; worker alienation in, 70, 87
"fairies" (homosexual class): toleration of, 115
fashion, male: photograph dating by, 30, 132, 135
females, 42; and effect of suffragists, on homophobia, 114; emasculating influence of, 87, 94, 96; romantic friendships in, 31, 34, 59. *See also* Smith-Rosenberg, Caroll
"Forty-niners": photographs of, 84, 86; romantic friendships among, 86–87
Foucault, Michel, 115
Fowler, Lorenzo, 99
Fowler, Orson, 99, 101, 106, 141
fraternal love, 60; among soldiers, 88; in Early Christian Church, 60; "Golden Age of" (Harwood), 94
fraternal organizations: as escape from mothers and wives, 87, 94, 96; ritualism in, 94, 96
Freud, Sigmund, 34, 42; on sex drive as universal motive force, 96, 98
friendship: and photographic portraiture as pledge of, 93
"friendship tradition," as social view of romantic friendships, 31, 34, 138. *See also* romantic friendships
Fritzinger, Warren, 144
frontier: as escape from industrialized workplace, 87; as escape from women's influence, 87; "Forty-niner" photographs, 84, 86; romantic friendships in, 34, 52, 86–87

Garrison, William Lloyd, 59, 60
Gay, Martin, 52, 55
Gay, Peter, 60, 108

gold rush: photographic images of, 84, 86; and romantic friendships, 86–87
Greeley, Horace, 63, 72, 93
Grimké, Angelina, 60

Halsey, Anthony, 62
Harned, Thomas, 148
Harwood, W. S., 94
Helen (mythology), 139
Hill (photographer), *117*
Hinojosa, Maria Antonia Cavazos de, 26
historians, queer: and role of, in validation of past, 51
historians, straight: and heterosexual categorization of same-sex love, 59
Holden, Charles W. (photographer), *68*
Holmes, Oliver Wendell, 70, 72, 90
Home-Treatment for Sexual Abuses: A Practical Treatise (Trall), 106
homophobia, 42; among collectors, 35, 36, 40–41; societal myths contributing to, 41–42; surge in (late 19th c.), 114
homosexuality, 50, 75; categorization of, as European invention, 56, 59; condemnation of, versus romantic friendship, 98–99, 106, 108, 110; "constructionist" view of, 56, 59; criminality of, 110, 114, 123; deterrence of, through normative sexuality, 115, 118; and "fairies," toleration of, 115; hellenistic references to, 60; and military policy, 123; as stage in social view of romantic friendship, 138; and straight historians on categorization of, 59; Victorian versus modern perspectives on, 56, 59, 62
Howe, George M., *17*
Humphrey's Journal, 93

Imperialist (newspaper), 118
Improved Order of Red Men, 94

Independent Order of Odd Fellows, 94
industrialization: and effect on artisanal way of life, 68–70; and worker alienation, 70, 87
"intimate friendships." *See* romantic friendships
Isaac (biblical name), 96
isolation, 72, 75, 86–87; and alienation, 70, 87; role of democracy in, 63; role of photograph to counter, 72, 75
Italia und Germania (Overbeck), 141, 143

Jackson, Andrew, 59, 69, 75, 101
Jefferson, Thomas, 63
Justitia (virtue), 138

Keenan, John A. (photographer), *37*
Kendall, Sergeant, 52
Kenedy, Mifflin, 26
King, Richard, 26
Knights of Pythias, 94

Labouchère Amendment, to Criminal Law Amendment Act (Great Britain), 110
Lambert, John, 52
La Salpêtrière (Paris hospital), 138
Lauren, Ralph, 19
Leaves of Grass (Whitman), 26, 28, 99, 115
Leda (mythology), 139
Lincoln, Abraham, 62
loneliness, 63, 86–87; and alienation, 70, 87; role of photograph to counter, 72, 75
"Lord's Supper" (da Vinci), 143
Lynch, Michael, 138, 141

marriage: and homophobic myths, 41; and male romantic friendships, 59, 60; and societal pressures, 42

COLLECTION CREDITS

★